CHRONICLES OF OLD ROME

EXPLORING ITALY'S ETERNAL CITY

© 2012 Tamara Thiessen

Published in the United States by:
Museyon, Inc.
20 E. 46th St., Ste. 1400
New York, NY 10017

Museyon is a registered trademark.
Visit us online at www.museyon.com

ISBN 978-0-9846334-4-9

1259611

Printed in China

*R*ome is part of the universal consciousness perhaps more than any other city in the world. For over 2,000 years, Roman culture has embedded itself into people's hearts and minds, starting with the footprint left by imperial Romans such as Caesar, Claudius and Hadrian: their baths, their aqueducts, their ancient temples and walls.

Visiting Rome, our craving to reconnect with the past—and the origins of civilization—is satiated.

Gazing at its enduring wonders, we can go back "to the source", as the Australian poet A. D. Hope wrote in his *Letter from Rome*.

"Yet here am I returning to the source.
The source is Italy, and hers is Rome.
The fons et origo *of Western Man.*

Like Goethe, who felt whole as a person for the first time in his life after his lengthy stays in the city in the 1780s, visitors can also feel an incredible sense of fulfillment from immersing in Rome's ancient wonders.

By wandering around this phenomenal outdoor museum—its mass of ancient, Renaissance and Baroque beauty—the soul is nourished, the mind enriched, and the sense of understanding of the past incredibly deepened.

—Tamara Thiessen

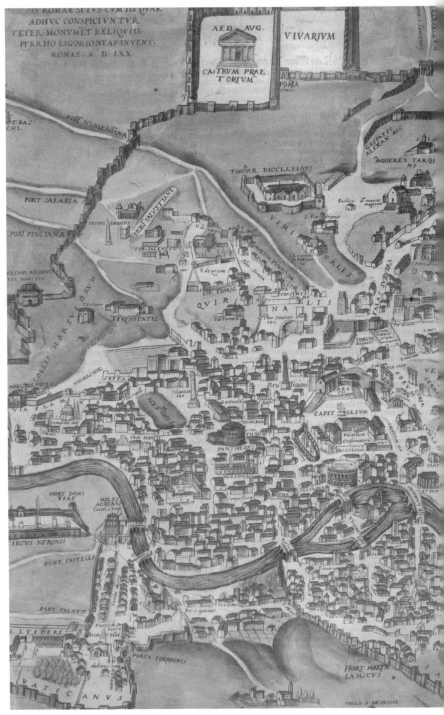

16th-century map of Rome

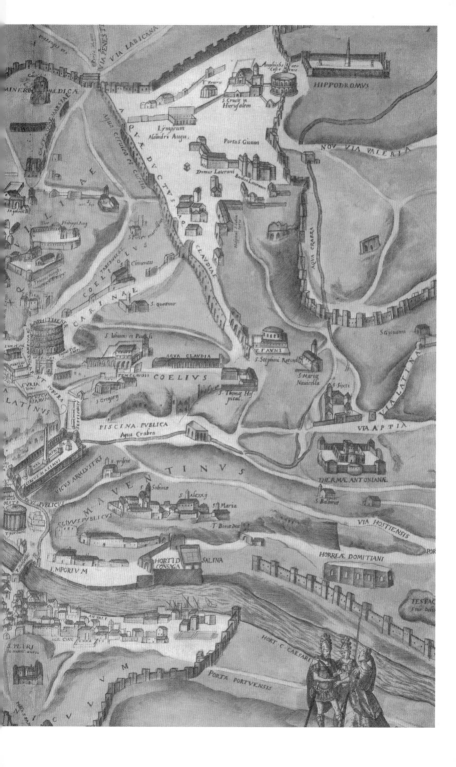

Gallery of Views of Ancient Rome, by Giovanni Paolo Panini, 1758,
Musée du Louvre

TIMELINE OF ROME HISTORY

753 B.C. Rome is founded by Romulus

509 B.C. Lucius Junius Brutus founds the Republic

300 B.C. Rome issues coins

218 B.C. Hannibal crosses the Alps and invades Italy

71 B.C. A slave, Spartacus, is killed and his rebel army is destroyed

51 B.C. Caesar conquers Gaul

44 B.C. Caesar becomes dictator for life and in March is murdered

31 B.C. Marcus Antony and Cleopatra are defeated by Octavian at battle of Actium

27 B.C. Augustus is made Rome's first emperor

. . . .

1 A.D. Rome's population reaches aproximately 1 million people

43 A.D. Romans invade Britain under Emperor Claudius

64 A.D. The Great Fire of Rome

80 A.D. The Colosseum is completed

126 A.D. Agrippa builds the Pantheon

139 A.D. Hadrian's mausoleum, Castel Sant' Angelo, is built

216 A.D. The Baths of Caracalla are built

312 A.D. Constantin I wins the Battle of Milvian Bridge

330 A.D. Capital moves from Rome to Constantinople (Istanbul)

c.360A.D. The First St. Peter's Basilica is consecrated

380 A.D. The Christian emperor Theodosius makes Christianity the official religion of Rome

395 A.D. Empire is divided into East and West

410 A.D. Rome is sacked by the Goths led by Alaric

452 A.D. Attila the Hun invades Italy–stays out of Rome on request of Pope Leo

455 Rome is sacked by the Vandals led by Gaiseric

476 The Western Empire falls

800 Charlemagne crowned Holy Roman Emperor

1309 The papacy is moved to Avignon under Pope Clement V

1347 The patriot and rebel Cola di Rienzo tries to restore the Roman Republic

1378 The papacy returns to Rome with Pope Gregory XI

1453 Byzantine Empire is defeated by Ottoman Turks

1508 Michelangelo starts painting in the Sistine Chapel

1527 Charles V's troops attack Rome, looting and ruining the city

1600 Giordano Bruno (philosopher) is burned at the stake for his heresies

1626 New St. Peter's Basilica is completed

1633 Galileo is condemned for heresy

1651 Piazza Navona is re-designed by Bernini

1798 Napoleon Bonaparte has Rome captured

1861 The Kingdom of Italy is founded with Turin as its capital

1870 Rome is made part of the Italian kingdom under Victor Emanuel II

1915 Italy enters World War I

1922 National Fascist Party rules Italy under Benito Mussolini

1929 A separate country, Vatican City, is created with the Lateran Treaty

1944 Rome is liberated by the Allied troops from the Germans

1960 Rome hosts the Olympic Games with great success

CHAPTER 1.

TALES OF ROME'S BEGINNING: AENEAS, ROMULUS, THE SHE-WOLF AND SEVEN HILLS

753 B.C.

At the center of the Sala della Lupa, the Wolf Room in Rome's Musei Capitolini, is a bronze statue of Rome's iconic she-wolf suckling the city's mythical founders, Romulus and Remus. The two bare-bottomed boys crouch beneath her teats, their palms upturned in cherubic rapture as providence flows down upon them. The *Lupa Capitolina*, donated to the people of Rome in 1471 by Pope Sixtus IV, was long thought to date to the early 5th century B.C., but carbon dating suggests she could be 1,000 years younger. Not possible, say critics, biting back on the hallowed wolf's behalf—Rome's symbol in the Middle Ages was a lion. Such speculation only adds to the mystique of Rome's beginnings.

Rome's history is a mesh of fantastic fable and fact. Tales of the city's beginning flow from the pen of Titus Livius, who began his monumental 142-book *History of Rome* in 27 B.C., under Rome's first emperor, Augustus. Written over four decades, the opus—of which thirty-five tomes survive—is widely acknowledged to blend truth and legend. Responding to critics with great foresight, Livy, as he is known, said embellishing history was a question of style, sparing the reader from "heavy and tedious" narrative. To accuse him of "violations of truth" would be absurd, he

The Capitoline She-Wolf with Romulus and Remus, Capitoline Museums

wrote—after all, he was simply retelling some of Rome's greatest legends, handed down through the ages from various sources.

The most popular of these legends is that of the twin brothers who battled each other for supremacy over the new city in 753 B.C., about two decades after being thrown into the Tiber River and suckled by a she-wolf. The wolf is Rome's most famous mascot—the surrogate mother of a city whose birth indisputably lies with the Tiber and the sweep of hills encircling it on the volcanic Latium plain.

The legend of the twins also links to that of the fabled exiled Trojan leader Aeneas, who fled the sack of Troy in the 11th century B.C. Borrowing from Homer's 8th-century B.C. Greek epic, *The Iliad*, ancient Romans adopted Aeneas as their own mythical ancestral hero.

After years of wandering, Aeneas is said to have built a town in the Roman countryside, calling it Lavinium, after his wife. "The region was called Latium, and the people there were termed Latins," wrote ancient historian Cassius Dio in his 80-book *Historia Romana*.

It was Aeneas's son, Ascanius, who would go on to found the ancient Latium city of Alba Longa, southeast of Rome. From his lineage sprung the legendary Romulus and Remus, and the Roman race.

The main thread of truth running through all the colorful stories of Rome's origins is the Tiber—as Livy exclaimed, the city's founding was all about location: "Not without reason did gods and men choose this spot…destined to grow great."

The history of the Eternal City has flowed down the Tiber, between its seven hills, separating Etruscan lands to the north and Latin Campania to the south.

Archeological evidence suggests rudimentary settlements existed on Rome's hills as far back as the 10th century B.C.—long before Romulus supposedly founded the city. Strategically located on the east side of the Tiber, between the Palatine and Esquiline hills, these small Latin camps, run by village chiefs, fell to the powerful Etruscans around 625 B.C.

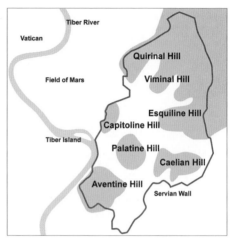

The Seven Hills of Rome

This still leaves room for a shred of truth in the legend of Romulus and Remus. According to Livy, the twins were the sons of a Vestal Virgin, Rhea Silvia, who was raped by the god Mars as she slept. Rhea was the daughter of Numitor, King of Alba Longa.

Numitor's brother, Amulius, had seized the throne, disposed of Numitor's son and forced Rhea to become a celibate priestess of the goddess Vesta, to prevent her producing a heir for Numitor.

When Amulius, the twins' great-uncle, learned of their birth, he was enraged, and buried Rhea alive for having broken her vow of chastity. Next he ordered his servant to throw Romulus and Remus in the Tiber. Instead, the slave set them afloat in a cradle—when it washed ashore, a thirsty she-wolf from the surrounding hills came to their aid. Wandering along the riverbank, Faustulus, a king's shepherd, found the wolf licking the boys and took the children home to his wife Acca Larentia, who raised them.

There is a twist in the wolf's tale. The "marvelous story" of the *lupa*, wrote Livy, may rest entirely with Larentia. An alternative version of the legend paints her as a prostitute, who was nicknamed the she-wolf for being "free with her favors" amongst Latium's shepherds. According to 2nd-century B.C. historian Cato the Elder, Larentia became wealthy plying her trade.

Aeneas's Flight from Troy, by Federico Barocci, 1598, Galleria Borghese

For her pivotal role in raising Romulus and Remus, she was made a Roman goddess—during the Larentalia festival on December 23, offerings were made to the dead at her shrine.

Yet another account claims Larentia was a mistress of Roman demigod and he-man Hercules, who advised her to marry the first man she met in the street, a wealthy Etruscan called Tarutius. Her husband died shortly after and left Larentia his vast estate, which she in turn bequeathed to Romulus and Roman citizens.

Fickle Roman fable has produced two famous foster moms—the she-wolf and Larentia—both of them deified for their nourishing, life-giving force in the city.

When Rome's riverbank twins grew up, wrote Livy, they helped restore their grandfather Numitor to his rightful throne in Alba by killing Amulius.

Determined to found their own city on the site they had been rescued and raised, their ambitions and "lust for royal power" sparked an "ugly struggle" between the brothers. Leaving it to the gods to choose the rightful ruler by way of omens, Romulus took up position on the Palatine and Remus on the neighboring Aventine. The appearance of vultures, circling in the sky above the neighboring hills, indicated the gods' decision.

Latin poet Ovid described the legend in his *Fasti*:

"No need for a fight to decide the issue," said Romulus:
"Much faith is put in the birds: Let us then try the birds."
All approved, and one to the cliff of the wooded Palatine went
at dawn to watch for birds, and the other climbed to the Aventine.

The first sign came to Remus, Livy wrote. "Six vultures—but they had no sooner announced the result than twice that number appeared to Romulus. Each of the camps claimed kingship for their leader, one side by virtue of priority and the other side by virtue of number."

With Romulus convinced that the gods' omen had been given to him, he began digging a trench around his new city. A fight broke out, and Remus was struck down and killed. Another common account of Rome's legendary fratricide says Remus mockingly jumped over his brother's new walls, which he had put in place to protect his city.

So it was Romulus who became the sovereign founder of Rome, and gave his name to the city. Ruling from 753 B.C. to 717 B.C., he was the first of seven kings on the Palatine, and may well have played a hand in federating the primitive Latin hilltop settlements into the "Septimontium," the forerunner of the famous seven-hilled city of Rome.

Rome's most cherished myths became major bricks and mortar in nation, or Empire, building—and for as long as Rome stands, to borrow the famous maxim about the Colosseum, so will the imprint of the she-wolf.

CHAPTER 2.

THE RAPE OF LUCRETIA: THE DAWN OF THE ROME REPUBLIC

508 B.C.

Around 508 B.C., so the legend goes, Lucretia, the benevolent, beautiful and virtuous wife of an aristocrat, was raped by Sextus Tarquinius, son of the Roman king. Her subsequent suicide spurred the Roman public to revolt, leading to the end of Lucius Tarquinius Superbus's tyrannical 25-year reign. The king and his family were banished from Rome, ending the long rule by a succession of Etruscan kings, who sprung from the region of Etruria, north of the city.

On the throne from 534–509 B.C., Tarquinius's reign began when he ordered the murder of his predecessor, Servius Tullius, and many of his supporters. This act paved the way, with blood, for his absolute power.

Early admiration for the king was quickly nullified by his "brutality and licentiousness," and his "wickedness and violence," wrote the ancient Rome-chronicler Titus Livy. He sapped public funds, forced indebted citizens into slavery and kept plebeians toiling "underground clearing out ditches and sewers."

Like many Roman rulers before and after him, the last thing Superbus had in mind was equality for his subjects, and his name beautifully captured his puffed up self-image—*Superbus*, the haughty one.

Extreme disregard for others ran in the family. According to the legend of Lucretia, the royal army was in the midst of besieging the neighboring Latin town of Ardea, to help bring some money back into Tarquinius's coffers, which had been impoverished by his grandiose public works.

Having failed in their assault, the Latins were thrown into a drawn-out war with the Rutilians of Ardea. During a furlough, a group of nobles gathered to feast and drink in the quarters of Sextus Tarquinius. Lucretia's husband, Lucius Tarquinius Collatinus, was one of those attending the party, at which the men began to brag about the relative merits of their wives.

"Heated with wine," wrote Livy, the group then decided to return to Rome and check in on their spouses by surprise, to test Collatinus's claims that his wife's virtuosity was matchless.

The king's daughters-in-law were all found feasting and partying with friends, while Lucretia was industriously spinning away at her loom.

Awarding her a palm of victory, as a model of wifely virtuosity, the Tarquin princes then spent the evening being entertained at the couple's home. "After their youthful frolic," wrote Livy, "inflamed by the beauty and exemplary purity of Lucretia," Sextus departed, determined to sully her purity and honor.

Several days later, knowing her husband was absent, Sextus returned to Lucretia's home on the pretext of a friendly visit. After supper, he was shown to the guest room, all the while plotting to carry out his dark plans of violating Lucretia's honor. When everybody was fast asleep, "he went in the frenzy of his passion with a naked sword to the sleeping Lucretia," wrote Livy, "and placing his left hand on her breast, said, Silence, Lucretia! I am Sextus Tarquinius, and I have a sword in my hand; if you utter a word, you shall die."

Crazed with brutal lust, he then subjected Lucretia at sword's point to a manipulative jumble of declarations of love and threats of death, in order to

Tarquinius and Lucretia, by Peter Paul Rubens, 1610,
The State Hermitage Museum, St. Petersburg

have his way with her.

Despite the tirade, Lucretia steadfastly rejected the prince's advances.

Humiliated and infuriated at his failure to vanquish her unflinching morality and fearless loyalty, Sextus threatened to disgrace Lucretia by slaying her servant then laying his naked body alongside hers, leading people to believe she had been killed for her adulterous actions.

He then proceeded to rape her, and left the house gloating victoriously about the "successful attack on her honor."

Crushed by a sense of shame, Lucretia sent for her father and husband, asking each of them to bring a witness to hear about the terrible incident. The group arrived to find a devastated Lucretia sitting in her room.

After listening to her tearful account, Collatinus tried to reassure his wife that it was "the mind that sins, not the body", but she remained inconsolable. Imploring the men to ensure that justice was served, she decided to set an example for all other women.

"Although I acquit myself of the sin, I do not free myself from the penalty," were the last words Lucretia spoke, according to Livy, before taking a knife concealed in her dress and plunging it into her broken heart.

Clutching the bloody knife, one of the witnesses, Lucius Junius Brutus— nephew of the king—swore to overturn the Etruscan monarchy.

Lucius Junius Brutus

Together they carried Lucretia's body to the Forum, where Brutus, the widely acknowledged founder of the Roman Republic, goaded "the incensed multitude" to revolt against Tarquinius, by invoking his uncle's countless atrocities and injustices.

After a decree was passed to strip the king of his sovereignty, Tarquinius Superbus and his family were shut out of the gates of Rome. The king, his wife and two of his sons fled to their Etruscan homeland.

Sextus Tarquinius, on the other hand, headed to Gabii, a Latin town that had refused to enter the Tarquin's confederation, where he mustered support by bad-mouthing his father. Initially, the people were tricked into appointing him as their leader, but when they realized that he planned to use the same tyrannical methods as his father, Sextus was murdered.

Back in Rome, Brutus was upheld as the liberator of the city, and 244 years of monarchic rule came to an end. With the overthrow of the tyrannical power of the Etruscan kings, came the dawn of the Roman Republic. Brutus and Collatinus became its first elected consuls, presiding over the sapling Senate.

For the next 500 years, the Senatus governed Rome, yet far from full-blown democracy, the council was dominated by the elite classes, who administered with a mix of dogmatism, consensus and oligarchy. It too, would falter in time, and the autocracy of the kings was outstripped by the long line-up of Roman emperors.

THE ENDURING LEGEND OF LUCRETIA

Lucretia, by Artemisia Gentileschi, c. 1621, Palazzo Cattaneo-Adorno, Genoa

Ever since the Latin poet Ovid uttered "Lucretia I have a blade, and I, a Tarquin, speak," her story has been a literary powerhouse, firing the imaginations of playwrights and poets, underpinning a Benjamin Britten opera, Shakespeare poems and Chaucer's tales of virtuous women.

In the 1660s, Rembrandt portrayed her in intense moments of despair, just before she takes her life and after she has plunged the knife into her heart.

A few decades earlier, Lucretia was one of the most important female subjects of Baroque painter Artemisia Gentileschi, who spent her life getting even with men through her paintings. Artemisia took a further stab at cherished male traditions by painting herself into the image of Lucretia, just as Caravaggio had done in many of his works, including *David with the Head of Goliath*.

Artemisia's bold, flesh-and-blood painting of Lucretia begs a question: Was the legend as pious as claimed, or did Rome's rulers turn her into a pin-up girl who was sacrificed allegorically as a lesson against adultery? Either way, she had been manhandled.

In accordance with her wish, Lucretia's valiant choice of death over dishonor set a stirring example, for men as well as women.

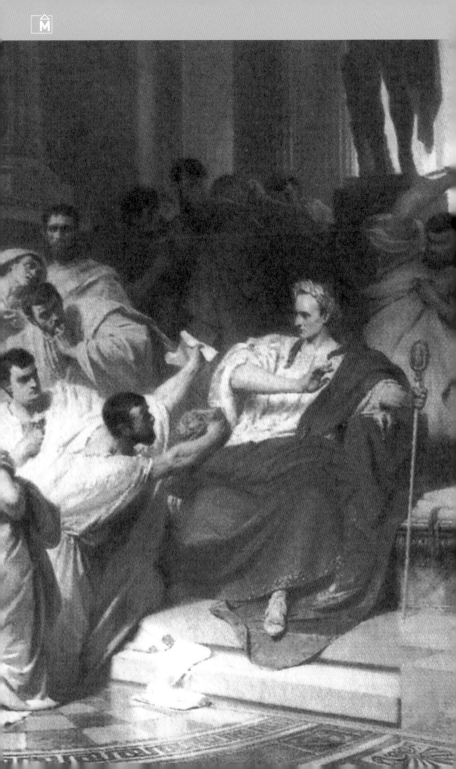

CHAPTER 3.

THE IDES OF MARCH: CAESAR'S DEMISE AT THE CURIA POMPEY

44 B.C.

On March 15, 44 B.C., Julius Caesar—the most famous Roman at home and abroad—was assassinated by a group of mutineer consuls in the Senate house, the Curia Pompeii. In a startling quirk of fate, his body slumped against a statue of Pompey the Great, his former political ally turned archrival, who fought the failed bid to stop Caesar becoming a dictator. Already renowned for his brilliantly masterminded conquests in Gaul and Britain, his resounding victory against Pompey's legions in 48 B.C. had put an end to civil war, and to the 500-year-old Republic—but within four years, the most talked about political murder in history brought his despotism to a halt.

Caesar had come ever so close to not attending the Senate on that fateful day, due to ill health and a flood of sinister premonitions. A soothsayer had warned Caesar the Ides of March spelled trouble. On March 14, a field martin had flown into the Curia with a laurel leaf and been ripped apart by a pack of predator birds. That evening, wrote historian Cassius Dio, Caesar dreamt he was flying "above the clouds," holding hands with Jupiter, while his wife, Calpurnia, envisioned him "stabbed in her arms."

‹ *The Murder of Caesar*, by Karl von Piloty, 1865, Lower Saxony State Museum, Hanover, Germany

23

The Death of Caesar, by Jean-Léon Gérôme, 1867, Walters Art Museum, Baltimore

Caesar's success had earned him many enemies, and he was well aware of the dangers that were lurking.

The Curia, where the murder took place, was part of Pompey's Theatre, built by the retired general in 55 B.C., as a lasting and spectacular reminder of his military achievements. Off its large colonnaded portico were several semi-circular halls, or *exedrae*, including the Curia Pompeii, which served as temporary meeting place for the Senate.

It was here the statesmen convened on March 14, as Caesar's Curia Julia— whose ruins stand in the Forum—was still under construction.

In his ancient biographies, Plutarch describes how Caesar's plotters first detained his loyal and physically powerful friend Mark Antony—who had caught wind of the stirrings the night before, and was on his way to join Caesar—outside in lengthy conversation.

When Caesar entered the hall, the Senate rose in his honor, but then a large group of dozens of conspirators encircled him like sharks, on the pretence of lobbying him on a political matter.

"Sitting down, Caesar tried to brush them off, but they continued to harass him with their request until Caesar was driven to show some violence of temper. It was then that Tillius gave the signal to begin the attack, jerking Caesar's toga down from both his shoulders," described Plutarch.

Julius Caesar

Over sixty of Caesar's adversaries, led by his brother-in-law, Cassius, and Pompey follower Brutus, had joined in the plot, motivated by a mix of Republican sentiment and personal dislike. The incensed, vicious mob stabbed the dictator twenty-three times. He surrendered to their hail of dagger blows, while prudently arranging his robe around the lower part of his body, in order to "fall more decently," wrote ancient biographer Gaius Suetonius Tranquillus in *The Twelve Caesars*.

His efforts did little to pretty up the death scene. Splattered head to toe in blood, he came to rest, slouched beside the effigy of his greatest enemy.

As Plutarch wrote, one might have thought that, "Pompey himself was presiding over this vengeance upon his enemy, who now lay prostrate at his feet, quivering from a multitude of wounds."

Caesar's body was carried on an ivory support to the Temple of Jupiter, on Capitoline Hill, for cremation among the gods; turned away by priests, Caesar's followers marched on to the Forum and placed the body outside his residence, the Regia, where his body was burned.

Immediate public frenzy over his death was quelled by propaganda from the Senate conspirators that it was all done in the name of democracy. Yet within no time, the powerful trio of Senate *triumvirs*—Octavian (Caesar's adopted son, later the Emperor Augustus), Mark Antony and Lepidus—started avenging his murder.

As well as purging political enemies under a guise of Senate legitimacy, they permanently walled up Pompey's Curia—which mourners had set fire to

Augustus of Prima Porta, 1 A.D.,
Vatican Museum

after Caesar's funeral—as a memorial to Caesar. The Second Triumvirate, as they were known (both Caesar and Pompey had been part of the First Triumvirate), also decreed the Senate would never again meet on March 15, in remembrance of the day of the bloody parricide.

By deifying Caesar, Octavian helped sanctify the much-loved ruler in the public memory—for Caesar had meant well in his efforts to rid Rome's political system of corruption, even if he had overstepped the mark.

As he famously declared to his general and faithful friend, Mark Antony, as they crossed the Rubicon river in 49 B.C. and rode back towards Rome: *alea iacta est*, the die is cast. Indeed, it was a point of no return, though Caesar wrongly believed Providence would always be on his side.

Since conquering the Gauls at the Battle of Alesia in 52 B.C., Caesar had slowly been angling to become supreme ruler of Rome. Cunningly rallying his army's support, he promised to use his office to free Rome from the hands of corrupt aristocrats who were ruling the Senate. As his aggressive dictatorial leadership spiralled, a splinter group of senators convinced Pompey to turn against his friend and lead Rome's legions to stop Caesar in his tracks.

They failed, up against Caesar's maverick warring instinct. Plutarch once marvelled at Caesar's ability to dictate several letters simultaneously, on horseback, during the Gallic campaigns. Against all odds, Caesar's famished army of 22,000 men thrashed Pompey's forces of 40,000 in the battle of Dyrrachium (in modern day Albania).

After two brief spells as dictator, in 44 B.C. Caesar assumed the role of ruler for life—*dictator perpetuus*—effectively becoming Rome's first emperor, without officially being declared one. With his dry humor, he jokingly rejected the suggestion of him assuming the title of king, saying that his name was Caesar—not *Rex* (King).

Besides, he already enjoyed a king's powers, conducting state affairs in a seat of ivory and gold, and treated by a largely adoring public as a god.

Yet Caesar's failure to deliver on his promises eventually caught up with him.

Instead of improving the lives of Romans, he deprived them of any shred of democracy, starting with the mistreatment of his own legions on the battlefield and culminating in his flagrant abuse of the Republican constitution, which ignited hatred and mistrust among a large group of senators. Getting rid of Caesar did not solve Rome's problems; the precedent for dictatorship was well off the starting block. In 27 B.C., tyranny became a way of life, with the beginning of five centuries of rule by Roman emperors.

Caesar had paved the way for the Empire with his military campaigns. As he wrote in a letter to a friend in Rome after one victory, *veni vidi vici*: "I came, I saw, I conquered." And that he did. In his time, Caesar is said to have conquered 300 nations and 800 cities, and defeated 3 million men.

Fast, aggressive and hot-headed, Pompey had rightly predicted that the same traits that underscored Caesar's strategic genius would also lead to his downfall. Caesar may nonetheless have had the last word over Pompey. When the Senate elected Octavian as the first emperor, he began his reign by removing the statue of Pompey in the Curia and destroying all busts and images of him and of Caesar's assassins.

CLEOPATRA, CAESAR, ANTONY AND AUGUSTUS

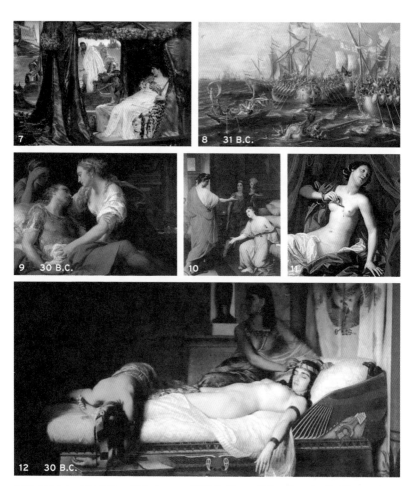

1. *Cleopatra,* by John William Waterhouse, c. 1887 2. *Caesar Giving Cleopatra the Throne of Egypt,* by Pietro da Cortona, c. 1637, Musée des Beaux-Arts, Lyon 3. *Cleopatra,* by Gustave Moreau, 1887, Musée du Louvre 4. *The Banquet of Cleopatra,* by Giovanni Battista Tiepolo, 1743–44, National Gallery of Victoria, Melbourne 5. *Cleopatra Testing Poisons on Condemned Prisoners,* by Alexandre Cabanel, 1887, Royal Museum of Fine Arts, Antwerp 6. *Cleopatra on the Terraces of Philae,* by Frederick Arthur Bridgman, 1896 7. *Antony and Cleopatra,* Lawrence Alma-Tadema, 1883 8. *The Battle of Actium,* by Lorenzo A. Castro, 1672, National Maritime Museum, Greenwich 9. *Cleopatra and the Dying Mark Antony,* by Pompeo Batoni, 1763, Musee des Beaux-Arts, Brest, France 10. *Cleopatra Being Captured by Octavian,* by Anton Mengs, 1770, Stourhead, England 11. *The Death of Cleopatra,* by Benedetto Gennari, 1686, Victoria Art Gallery, Bath 12. *The Death of Cleopatra,* by Jean Andre Rixens, 1874, Musée des Augustins, Toulouse

CHAPTER 4.

FREE AND NOT SO FREE SPEECH: CICERO AT THE FORUM

43 B.C.

In the 1st century B.C., the Roman Forum was a political and public theater for the Latin art of oration. In the crowded meeting place, plebs gathered to witness laws being passed and to vote for publicly elected tribunes. The speaker's *rostra*, or podium, put the *oratori* center stage as they harangued the masses on burning issues, and pleaded cases of morality and justice.

Romans loved a good speech, and no one delivered them better than Cicero.

Marcus Tullius Cicero spoke often at the Forum during his career as lawyer, statesman and scholar of ancient Rome, and his forceful, emotive and witty war of words pitted him against powerful allegiances in the Senate.

Ultimately, the orator was to pay a heavy price for speaking out.

Cicero considered the Forum a public university in the art of eloquence. He learned "to fight in the very thick of the throng," wrote Victorian-era novelist, Anthony Trollope, in The *Life of Cicero*, judging that Cicero's mastery of Latin made it "so graceful in prose, and so powerful a vehicle of thought."

Marcus Tullius Cicero

The *rostra* from which Cicero dazzled the crowd, lay alongside the Curia Hostilia, the Senate House, whose politicians were a major inkwell for Cicero's vitriol.

Witnessing the disintegrating values of the Roman Republic through the dictatorships of Sulla and Caesar, Cicero tried in vain to put a stop to the tyranny with his sizzling eloquence and lively arguments.

"It is for their own power men are fighting now to the danger of the country," he wrote to his friend Atticus, as the 49 B.C. Civil War between Caesar and Pompey broke out.

His role model was Demosthenes, the famous Greek orator who talked with pebbles in his mouth to overcome a childhood stutter, recited verses while running, and spoke over the roar of waves to strengthen his voice. Demosthenes's invective against Philip of Macedon, the *Philippic*, became a sobriquet for damning political discourses.

Cicero increasingly used this style, and his mordant missives often took aim at Roman consuls.

His fourteen *Philippics* against Mark Antony, written between 44–43 B.C., got him into deep, and scorching, water. The first of these denunciations of Mark Antony's "treason and insane policy"—the *oratio Philippica prima*—was addressed to the Senate in Antony's absence on September 2, 44 B.C.

Enraged by the speech, Antony replied on September 19th with a vicious slur against Cicero, implicating him in the plot to assassinate Caesar.

Cicero lashed back with the second and most damning philippic, circulated as a pamphlet late in November but never presented to the Senate. In the text, Cicero lampoons Antony's public and private vices; his detrimental impact on the republic and criminal squandering of money; his drunken, avaricious, arrogant, womanizing behavior; and his stocky gladiator's body.

Cicero Denounces Catiline, by Cesare Maccari, 1889, Palazzo Madama, Rome

At the time, Cicero and Antony were the most popular men in Rome, the former holding fast to republican values, the latter set on avenging Caesar's murder.

Two camps developed in the Senate. Cicero sided with Octavian—Caesar's 18-year-old great-nephew—for whom Antony was also a bitter rival in his rise to become Rome's first emperor. Octavian admired Cicero, describing him as a man "who loved his country well."

Antony and Octavian temporarily put their differences aside to form the Second Triumvirate of all-powerful senators, along with the Roman general Lepidus. The trio immediately drew up an official inventory of their enemies, and despite Octavian's resistance, Antony put Cicero's name high on the list.

The verbal marksman, having doggedly attacked Antony, now had a price put on his head.

On December 7, 43 B.C., Antony's men caught up with Cicero as he tried to escape along the coastal road between Rome and Naples, near the promontory of Caieta (now the Gulf of Gaeta).

Cicero had retreated hastily to his seaside holiday home at Vindicium with his servants, as the heat turned up on him in Rome. As Cicero arrived by boat, a flight of crows hovered noisily around his vessel, wrote Plutarch in his ancient Greek and Roman biographies, *Parallel Lives*. "All looked upon this as an ill omen; yet Cicero went on shore." As Cicero lay down to rest, "a number of the crows settled in the chamber-window, and croaked in the most doleful manner." One of the birds landed on the bed, and tried with its beak to remove the clothes with which Cicero was concealing his face.

After debating whether to stay and witness their master's undoing, the servants started carrying Cicero back towards the sea on a litter (the Roman equivalent of a sedan chair), as the assassins approached through the forest. Commanding the search team were the centurion Herennius and Popilius Laenas, a plebeian magistrate who Cicero had once defended in court, not only freeing him from murder charges with the power of his eloquence, but sparing his life.

Having tried in vain to flee, Cicero was left to face his fate.

"There is nothing proper about what you are doing, soldier, but do try to kill me properly," were the orator's last words, before he bared his neck to Herennius, who cut off his head, and, on Antony's clear instructions, the hands used to pen the offensive *Philippics*.

Such a sorry sight was Cicero in his last moments, his miserable face "overgrown with hair, and wasted with anxiety," wrote Plutarch, that Herennius's attendants "covered their faces during the melancholy scene."

Antony ordered the head and hands be nailed on the *rostra*, where Cicero had spoken out against him on so many occasions.

In full public view, Cicero was left to "moulder there in mockery of the triumphs of his eloquence," wrote William Forsyth in *Life of Marcus Tullius Cicero*. The sight of his dismembered head made many a Roman shudder, for they imagined they were looking at the "image of the soul of Antony"—a blackened soul at that—rather than the face of Cicero, wrote Plutarch.

Before his remains were displayed for all to see, Antony's wife, Fulvia—

Fulvia With the Head of Cicero, by Pavel Svedomsky

who was once married to another of Cicero's enemies—vented her hatred on the dead orator by spitting on his remains. Even that was not enough to satiate her appetite for revenge. Next, she took the head, placed it on her lap, pried open the mouth and proceeded to jab and pierce the tongue "that had argued so eloquently against her husband" with her hair pins, wrote ancient chronicler Cassius Dio.

Tickled pink with his role in the murder, Popilius "set up a statue of himself wearing a wreath, sitting beside the severed head of Cicero," Dio wrote. This gesture pleased the vengeful Mark Antony to such a point that he added a bonus to the reward Popilius was to receive for Cicero's head.

As though trying to out-match his wife's ugly payback, Antony's attentions next turned to Philologus, a freedman and former slave of Cicero's brother, Quintus Cicero.

Philologus—one of Cicero's former Latin pupils—had betrayed the orator to the tribune by leading the execution party to him in the forest. "Perversely," wrote Dio, Antony had Philologus delivered to Cicero's sister-in-law, Pomponia, who forced him to cut off his own flesh bit by bit, roast it and eat it.

CHAPTER 5.

THE LATIN LOVER: OVID'S MANUAL OF SEDUCTION

25 B.C.

In the flourishing literary world of the Augustan age, the Latin poet Ovid was on a trail to fame with lusty lines that taught seduction techniques for both sexes. From smuggling love letters in bosoms and sexual stances to concealing stretch marks and saggy breasts, his tips titillated the Roman reader. But the adulterous promiscuity promoted in his *Ars Amatoria* (The Art of Love) hit too close to home for morally-crusading Emperor Augustus, who banished Ovid.

The Golden Age of Latin literature was a period of vigorous state patronage of writers and poets between 80 B.C. and 14 A.D. Among its string of luminaries—Horace, Virgil, Livy—Publius Ovidius Naso was the first to live his life wholly in the Augustan Empire.

Born in 43 B.C., he enjoyed a brief career as a brilliant, elegant young lawyer, before plunging head first into poetry in his early twenties. Starting with *Amores*, a series of poems addressed to his fictional mistress Corinna, his works were spicy, saucy declarations on love, sex and seduction. Writing in elegiac verse sparkling with wit and frivolity, he proved himself a literary flirt *par excellence*.

Love Scene, 1st century A.D.,
Kunsthistorisches Museum, Vienna

"When, her apparel laid aside, she stood naked before mine eyes, not a blemish was to be seen on her whole body," he wrote in Book 1, Elegy V of *Amores*, entitled "His delight at having obtained Corinna's Favours."

"What shoulders, what arms, it was my privilege to behold and to touch...Wearied, we rested from our toil. May many an afternoon be thus sped by."

Ars Amatoria, written in 2 B.C., outshone his previous works by elaborating the nitty-gritty mechanisms of the love game. In reality, the text was about the art of promiscuity, audaciously teaching readers how to go about conquering the object of their desire, and encouraging wicked liaisons and unbridled libertinism. The world's first how-to guide to seduction comprised three books of verse, the first two aimed at men, the third at women. Both were aphrodisiac-laden prescriptions for unleashing more than just hearts.

Proclaiming himself the "master in Love's mighty school," Ovid implores those undertaking his degree in seduction to not waste a second, and just go out and get 'em.

Like a general training the Roman legions in the Campus Martius to go into battle, in Book 1 Ovid likens the pursuit of a woman to hunting, and women as fair game. Seduction is not something to be left to spontaneity and starry-eyed encounters: The perfect damsel "drops not from the sky; She must be sought for with a curious eye...First seek an object worthy of your flame; then strive, with art, your lady's mind to gain."

Coaching his students on calculating love strategies, he makes love out to be a battle: Having armed the men "for the fight prepare," it was now time to "arm the fair."

Entrance to a Roman Theatre, by Lawrence Alma-Tadema, 1866

The third book not only instructs women how to seduce men, but also encourages them to live a lustful life before they lose their looks and youth: "How soon a wrinkled skin plump flesh invades!"

Despite some forgivably conservative ideas on gender roles, he finds men are often liars, and urges young "nymphs" to stay free of the confines of marriage, and to make the most of the chance to "try young and older lovers."

Furthermore, he gives women tips on ways to deceive men—using jealousy and fear to get the upper hand, or playing "cloak and dagger" to add intrigue to waning romance.

As for delivering those naughty missives, he suggests a "knowing maid can carry letters you've penned, concealed in the deep curves of her warm breasts."

To both men and women he provides copious advice on grooming—though this is no metrosexual society, and men are warned not to overdo it—no hair curling wands or leg-waxing, boys, work on the tan and the gym instead.

Women should make themselves coquette with makeup, and in the poem *Medicamina Faciei Femineae*, or Makeup for a Woman's Face, Ovid even recommends facial treatments made of barley, eggs, stag's horn, narcissus bulbs, Tuscan seed and honey.

In *Ars Amatoria*, he also provides an inventory of the best pick-up places in Rome: The Roman theaters, especially the airy patios and arcades attached to them such as Pompey's Portico, are ideal cruising or "hunting" spots, advises Ovid. At the playhouses, the games, even at the synagogues on the

Ovid among the Scythians, by Eugène Delacroix, 1859, National Gallery, London

Sabbath, men will find plenty of available and desirable female "prey," either for a passing dalliance or longer "fondle and caress."

In the event that his counseling backfired, and cupid gained the upper hand, the scribacious scoundrel of sexual conquest, of broken hearts and impish advice, wrote a sequel.

In *Remedia Amoris* (Cures for Love), he offers a collection of timeless instructions on how to "have more than one lover," "be cool" or "sate yourself with her," "forget her," "get rid of all reminders" and "love your rival."

Within six years of the publication of *Ars Amatoria*, Emperor Augustus— once a strong admirer—banished Ovid to Tomis on the Black Sea, where he spent the last decade of his life.

Why did this work promote such outrage from the emperor, when a decidedly sexually lenient society had already lapped up a string of his sassy epistles?

Augustus's whole reign was spent trying to restore traditional family values to a morally decaying Rome. While sexual liberty was permissible up to a point, Ovid's poem flagrantly flouted the law against adultery.

The timing could not have been worse.

In the same year *Ars Amatoria* was written, Augustus had banished his daughter Julia to Pandateria—an island in the Bay of Naples—because of her "nocturnal debaucheries." He also exiled, or executed, numerous young aristocrats with whom she had been behaving bawdily.

In a double whammy of humiliation, the Emperor had to deal with a morally loose daughter and a provocative poet—so much for his efforts to restore morality.

Ovid, it would seem, rubbed salt into the wounds by offering personalized guidance to adulterers. "As the author of a vile poem, I am charged with being a teacher of obscene adultery," he wrote in his sorrowful poems from exile, *Tristia*.

The fact that Ovid had cleverly "decked his poem with fig-leaves here and loopholes there," through the use of irony, says British author and Ovid translator Tom Payne, did little to detract from its outrageous literary licentiousness and libido.

For authoring a romantic and erotic tour de force, Ovid became a moral martyr.

CHAPTER 6.

CALIGULA'S NEEDLE: THE VATICAN OBELISK
37 A.D.

From temples dedicated to Isis to towering symbols of the sun god, Rome's Egyptomania was on show throughout the Empire after its conquest of Egypt in 30 B.C. Obelisks and other monuments taken from temples, or offered as gifts, loomed high over the city as status symbols. Today these granite behemoths sanctifying the sun stand at striking odds with the city's Christian trappings; none more so than Caligula's obelisk, now in St. Peter's Square. Getting it to Rome was a monumental effort.

Egypt's seduction of Rome started with Cleopatra and her political and passion-fueled affair with Julius Caesar. After his arrival in Egypt with his troops in 48 B.C., Cleopatra made a beeline towards Caesar, seeking his help to solve the dynastic dispute between her and her brother, King Ptolemy XIII, which had forced her into exile.

After sneaking her way across the harbor into Alexandria, then into Caesar's royal quarters wrapped in a carpet, the 21-year-old conquered the 52-year-old Caesar as an ally and a lover.

The affair produced a son, Caesarion, or "little Caesar," who, as a 13-year-

Cleopatra and Caesar,
by Jean-Leon-Gerome, 1866

old, ruled Egypt with his mother, at the instigation of her new lover Mark Antony, who she seduced during his mission to modern day Turkey in 41 B.C.

Determined that first impressions never die, Cleopatra sailed into Tarsus, dressed as Venus, "in a barge with gilded stern and outspread sails of purple, while oars of silver beat time to the music of flutes and fifes and harps," wrote ancient Greek historian Plutarch. "Lying beneath a canopy of gold cloth," she was fanned by cherubic boys and attended by maids, "garbed as sea nymphs." The word spread fast "that Venus had come to feast with Bacchus, for the common good of Asia."

The immortal story of the famous Roman consul and Egyptian queen is one of illegitimate children, secret marriages, fratricide and switching political allegiances.

Sparks were already flying between Antony and Caesar's nephew, Octavian (the future emperor Augustus), after Antony abandoned his wife Octavia—Octavian's recently widowed sister, whom he had offered in marriage to strengthen their alliance—for Cleopatra. When Antony started giving away bits of the Empire to Cleopatra and the three children they had spawned, a fed-up Octavian declared war on Egypt.

After their defeat in the naval Battle of Actium in 31 B.C., Antony plunged himself onto his sword as Alexandria fell to the Romans. Nine days later, Cleopatra poisoned herself with the bite of an Egyptian cobra, brought to her in a basket of figs. After the suicides, Octavian had Caesarion killed.

With Egypt netted into the Roman Empire, obelisks became a desirable monument to adorn ceremonial places, and emperors engaged in a similar obelisk power show to the Egyptian kings.

Caligula

For the Egyptians, the tall tapering pillars linked sky and earth and symbolized the pharaoh's divine right to rule. "They designated these obelisks as sacred to the Sun-god, and indeed their shape is a symbol of the sun rays, signified by the Egyptian word for obelisk—*tekhen*—meaning both obelisk and ray of light," wrote 1st-century historian Pliny the Elder in his *Historia naturalis*.

In ancient Rome, the Egyptian obelisks were a take-home keepsake of imperial conquests.

The first emperor to bring one to Rome was Caligula in 37 A.D. The notorious emperor transported it from Heliopolis, the Egyptian center of sun worship, at the beginning of his dramatic four-year rule.

Within that time, culminating in his murder, he ruined the empire with his squandering, according to the contemporary Roman philosopher Seneca, and became notorious for his sexual perversity and irrational, cruel ways.

During his reign, Caligula had three wives, infamously made his favorite horse, Incitatus, a senator, and developed an increasingly mad god complex, impersonating various deities from Hermes to Apollo. Brandishing thunderbolts, he replaced the heads of statues of gods with his own and even considered committing the major offence of having one such statue installed in the temple in Jerusalem.

With the nickname that had stuck since childhood—Caligula, or "little boots"—Gaius Julius Caesar's short-lived popularity slid disastrously due to his excessive spending on entertainment, and his corruption. Within a year he bled dry a legacy of "two thousand seven hundred million" *sesterces* left by his predecessor and great-uncle, Tiberius, according to Suetonius in his *Lives of the Caesars*. He started robbing from Romans, by devising shifty tax schemes, stealing from their estates and rigging auctions. At one public sale, a praetorian guard unwittingly acquired thirteen gladiators for a vast sum of money; several of those ruined by Caligula committed suicide.

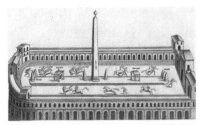

Top: *Circus Neroni* (Cirucus Vaticanus), by Pietro Santi Bartoli, 1699; bottom: *Church of Santa Maria della Febbre*, by Pieter Jansz Saenredam, 1629. The church of Santa Maria della Febbre stood on the former site of the Circus Vaticanus beside the Vatican obelisk before its 1585 move.

Posing as Neptune or Jupiter, he would seduce women, including his sisters, and cross-dressed as goddesses such as Venus and Diana, wearing wigs and accessories. Appearing in public "in silk or in triumphal dress," wrote Dio, he extended either his hand or his foot to senators, for them to kiss in homage.

As a symbol of his surging potency, Caligula wanted an obelisk to grace the arena he was building on Vatican Hill.

Getting it to Rome was no easy feat. According to Pliny, it took up to 120,000 men to build an obelisk—the toughest part, however, lay in relocating, not quarrying, these monoliths.

The Egyptians had worked out ways of moving obelisks on the Nile—the greatest challenge in shipping Caligula's obelisk from Egypt to Rome, then up the Tiber from the coast, was finding a suitable ship for the cargo. Caligula had a vessel expressly built for the task—"Fortunately," wrote Pliny, "the [Tiber] river has just as deep a channel as the Nile."

Its arrival in Rome was a spectacular sight. Entering the harbor of Rome, at Ostia, "with a ballast of 120 bushels of lentils", the hulk took up nearly half of the port. "It is certain that nothing more wonderful than this ship has ever been seen on the sea," wrote Pliny.

The eye-catching obelisk was erected at the center of Caligula's stadium—on the *spina*, a dividing wall typically reserved for monuments and statues.

The so-called Circus Vaticanus started as a humble, private racetrack, in which Caligula exercised his passion for charioteering by organizing races

The Moving of the Vatican Obelisk, by Domenico Fontana, c. 1590

amongst his favorite horses and riders, and spending hours hanging out around the stables. Chariot racing was subject to spectator fanaticism in ancient Rome, between fans of four deeply divided factions—the greens, the whites, the reds and the blues. Caligula, a zealous supporter of the green racing team, was known to poison both rival horses and charioteers, according to Cassius Dio.

Though it was "half sunk in the earth", the 85-foot red granite monolith was still standing upright 1,500 years later, apparently spared from the fate that befell other pagan shrines. In 1585, Pope Sixtus V gave engineer Domenico Fontana the incredibly difficult task of moving the mammoth obelisk to the Piazza San Pietro. It took him and 800 workers nearly a year to accomplish. The second highest of Rome's obelisks after the 105-foot Lateran Obelisk, the Vatican Obelisk features none of the usual hieroglyphic engravings, but it does have Latin inscriptions on its base.

Its placement before St. Peter's Basilica owes to the saint; Christians believe he was crucified at the Circus Vaticanus during Nero's time. In a further twist in the tale of the obelisk's switch from pagan to Christian symbol, Roman legend long held that Caesar's ashes were enshrined in a bronze ball at the top of "St. Peter's needle."

CHAPTER 7

EMPRESS WITH AN IRON GRIP: AGRIPPINA THE YOUNGER

59 A.D.

Mother of an emperor, sister of an emperor, wife of an emperor and suspected murderer of an emperor, Agrippina the Younger was born into the hornet's nest of the Julio-Claudian dynasty, which produced Rome's first five emperors. Her brother Caligula and son Nero are cited among her many lovers and Claudius, her third husband, was her uncle. Evoking the Italian word *grippare*, to seize, her name captures her ambitious, fiery character and the manner in which, as a woman, she wielded unprecedented power over the Roman Empire. Until, that is, her son Nero took care of her.

Julia Agrippina was born around 15 A.D. into a dysfunctional dynasty—her father Germanicus had been adopted by Emperor Tiberius, who allegedly had his three sisters married off after he had raped them.

When Agrippina became the fourth wife of Britain's invader, Claudius, in 49, the marriage meant a return to the Palatine Hill. As an 11-year-old, she lived there with Caligula and her sisters in the Casa di Livia, the home of her great-grandmother Livia Drusilla—Rome's first Empresses, Julia Augusta. The house was by many accounts a dark, scary place, seething with tension.

Shortly after he arrived in power in 14 A.D., her adoptive grandfather Tiberius had built the Domus Tiberiana, a 160,000-square-foot add-on to all the previous imperial residences. (Though covered in the mid-15th century by the Orti Farnesiani gardens, remains of its 20-meter-high arched walls still peep from the hillside above the Roman Forum.)

It was here that Agrippina lived with Claudius. Once settled in the palace, she immediately ordered further showy extensions to the residence, and "gained complete control of Claudius," wrote 2nd-century historian, Cassius Dio. She henpecked Claudius, wrote Dio, "for she possessed in an unusual degree, the quality of *savoir faire*."

On the evening of October 12, 54 A.D., there was much feasting going on at the Domus Tiberiana. The merriment may have been part of a festival honoring the first Emperor Augustus, Julia Agrippina's late great-grandfather.

Sometime between the night of the 12th and noon the following day, in the midst of the banqueting bash, Claudius dropped dead. Though many believe he died from poisoned mushrooms, conjecture over the circumstances of his death has reigned much longer than Claudius did.

The emperor's family and other dining company apparently hardly noticed him dying—they were so accustomed to seeing him debauched. With Claudius almost prostrate over his plate of mushrooms, his physician Stertinius Xenophon treated him for symptoms of heartburn, by applying a "feather to the fauces"—that is tickling his throat to induce vomiting.

The powerful physician, who managed the medical affairs of emperors Caligula, Claudius and Nero, earned his place in medical history through his connections with the wealthy and unscrupulous, more than for his professional credentials.

Most ancient historians believed Agrippina and her doctor friend were guilty. Treating Claudius for indigestion was a mere pretext, they argued, a second attempt to kill him after the plate of poisoned mushrooms failed. Acting on Agrippina's orders, the doctor slipped a feather dipped in monkshood—a deadly and fast-working poison—in the emperors' throat.

The Death of Messalina by Georges Antoine Rochegrosse, 1916

Single-mindedly obsessed with getting her son Nero into power, Agrippina mercilessly drove away any rivals, and murder was one option in her bag of evil tricks.

In 51 A.D., Agrippina had persuaded Claudius to adopt Nero, thus giving him precedence as heir apparent over Claudius's younger son, Britannicus. The powerful and manipulative Empress now wanted her husband out of the picture, wrote her contemporary Pliny the Elder, before dealing with Britannicus.

Named in memory of his father's conquests in Britain, Britannicus's mother was 15-year-old Valeria Messalina, commonly portrayed as a teenage nymphomaniac, who used to slip away from the Domus Tiberiana in disguise for her nightly revels. Though tales of endless orgies were no doubt exaggerated, Messalina's escapades were real enough for Claudius to have his third wife executed for adultery.

Undoubtedly, Claudius would have done the same with Agrippina if he had known what she had in store for him. Following his death Agrippina kept her son almost under house arrest at the Domus Tiberiana. In his annals, Cornelius Tacitus wrote Agrippina even offered herself to her "half intoxicated son" on several occasions, in a desperate bid to maintain her grip.

Nero may also have been an accomplice in Claudius's murder, enlisting the help of Locusta, a professional poisoner renowned for her seedy trade in deadly potions.

Nero raised suspicions by laughing out loud over a play written by his adviser, the Roman playwright Seneca, within months of Claudius's demise. The play sends up the emperor's fate, by having him die while being entertained by a group of comic actors. Instead of being deified, he is pumpkinified, or gourdified, as the play's title *Apocolocyntosis* signifies.

Within a year there was another poisoning on the Palatino. Britannicus, like his father, was murdered during a feast laid on by the recently inaugurated 17-year-old Emperor Nero, not long after Agrippina had successfully maneuvered him into absolute power in 55 A.D.

Agrippina's time would soon come. Sick of her meddling in his personal affairs, and taunted by his girlfriend Poppaea for being under his mother's thumb, Nero planned her murder in 59 A.D., during a festival at the posh Roman resort of Baiae in the Gulf of Naples.

Having arranged a reception in Agrippina's honor at a villa at nearby Bauli, Nero encouraged his mother to take an evening cruise. After banqueting until after midnight with friends, the revelers went down to the shore to witness Agrippina being castaway, unwittingly, in a vessel rigged with a collapsible lead ceiling.

The ploy failed. Instead of sinking the ship, the canopy crushed one of Agrippina's servants, Crepereius Gallus. Agrippina herself, who was reclining on a couch on deck, was saved by the height of the couch, wrote Tacitus.

The whole episode turned into a fiasco, with those crew members who were aware of the conspiracy trying to capsize the boat, and those who were not

Nero and the Corpse of Agrippina, by Pietro Negri, c. 1629-79

acting as ballast. In the scuffle, Agrippina fell into the water and managed to swim to shore, despite having consumed a considerable amount of food and wine.

In the early hours, Nero's henchmen caught up with her at her villa. Pooh-poohing their suggestion that she was to be murdered on her beloved son's orders, she thrust the womb that bore an emperor towards her assassins, and cried: "Strike here." With that, a centurion ended her life with a sword, at the age of 43.

"Her body was burnt that same night on a dining couch," wrote Tacitus. Some say Nero gazed at her naked corpse and praised her beauty ahead of her cremation, and both Tacitus and Dio testify to Agrippina's attractiveness.

Opinion is deeply split between those who paint Nero as a victim of a cruel, controlling mother, and those who consider Agrippina a casualty of history, her story clouded by myth and bias.

Just like other "bad girls" of the Empire, her image may have been distorted by smear campaigns. It was common for rivals to use tales of teenage nymphomaniacs, wicked stepmothers and incestuous, bossy empresses to discredit the regime, and many of those stories have stuck. There is still plenty of proof of the Julio-Claudian depravity for it to be believed—even Agrippina's own memoirs, recounting the misfortunes of her family, informed ancient historians, though they have since been lost.

Producing one of the greatest monsters of the Empire may have been her undoing, but it was also her crowning glory. Warned by astrologers that Nero would not only be emperor, but also kill her, she answered, "Let him... provided he is emperor."

CHAPTER 8.

DOMESTIC BLISS: NERO'S GOLDEN HOUSE
64 A.D.

While the first emperor, Augustus, chose a humble abode in line with his subtle dictatorial style, later rulers knew no such modesty. The hill on which Romulus supposedly found Rome was a potent symbol for future despots keen on demonstrating their supremacy. Their palaces were status symbols, smothered in precious statues, stones and frescos. Nero's new quarters outshone them all.

One of Rome's notoriously mad and bad emperors, Nero came to power on a bloody trail of family plotting and poisonings, and ruled Rome in the same sinister way. Aided and abetted by an overbearing mother, his "career of parricide and murder," as Nero's near contemporary Suetonius described the reign in his *Lives of The Twelve Caesars*, began with the murder of his stepfather, the Emperor Claudius, "for even if he was not the instigator of the emperor's death, he was at least privy to it, as he openly admitted." Once in power, Nero "showed neither discrimination nor moderation in putting to death whomsoever he pleased on whatever pretext."

According to Suetonius, Nero murdered dozens by having a physician cut their veins, in a similar manner to which he himself committed suicide. He

‹ The *Laocoön*, now at the Vatican Museums, was discovered amid the ruins of Nero's Domus Aurea.

55

The Fire of Rome, 18 July 64 A.D., Hubert Robert, 1785, Musée des Beaux-Arts Andre Malraux, Le Havre

also kept an Egyptian slave, "who would crunch raw flesh and anything else that was given him." Nero apparently enjoyed throwing the glutton "live men to be torn to pieces and devoured."

Fuelled by an unscrupulous mania for collecting, Nero hoarded treasures of the empire in his lavish new abode—a "home shining with the glitter of gold" that was built immediately after the Great Fire of 64 A.D. destroyed more than half the city.

Far from a new beginning, it was the beginning of the end for the 27-year-old emperor, who had already been on the throne for ten years.

No sooner than the ashes of the fire had settled, wrote the historian Tacitus, Nero quickly "availed himself of his country's desolation" and built a new home in the center of Rome, yet surrounded by fields, forest and water "to resemble a wilderness." The sprawling complex, hemmed in by vineyards and meadows, was filled with treasures sacked from cities of the Orient and precious ornaments.

On the emperor's orders, homes and public buildings were demolished to make way for the immense palace and its waterfalls, zoos, statue parks, private bathing complex and amphitheater. Extending over nearly 200 acres between the Palatine and Oppian hills, it had "buildings as big as whole towns" and a vast lake, the Stagnum Neronis, "almost like a sea." To fill the artificial lake, which was located in the valley now filled by the Colosseum, Nero foolishly attempted to sink a 160-mile canal through the hills to the mouth of the Tiber in Ostia.

The palace was a monument to Nero's narcissist follies, notably his

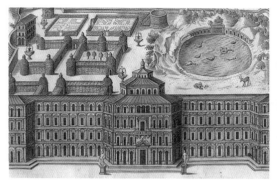

Left: *Golden House of Nero and its Gardens,* by Pietro Santi Bartoli, c. 1690
right: *The Great Hall of Domus Aurea* (artist's reconstruction), by G.Chedanne (1861-1940)

unrestrained plunder of priceless *objet d'art* to fill the residence. His hive of hedonism dripped with marble, mother-of-pearl and so much gold leaf it was christened Domus Aurea, the golden house.

Suetonius describes the "mad extravagance" of the 150-room, 370-meter-long residence, with its halls and walls clad in colored stucco, paintings of nymphs and frescos illustrating epic Greek poems and legends. "There were dining-rooms with fretted ceils of ivory, whose panels could turn and shower down flowers and were fitted with pipes for sprinkling the guests with perfumes. The main banquet hall was circular and constantly revolved day and night, like the heavens."

In 2009, archeologists found what they believe are remains of Nero's revolving dining room, the *"coenatio rotunda"*, on the Palatine. The perpetually rotating room, nearly 200 feet long, was a feat of Roman engineering. Perched on top of a massive pillar, it was spun around by an under-the-floor mechanism of water-powered gyrating cylinders.

Nero's art raids in Greece turned his *domus* into a museum of Classical and Hellenistic masterpieces. Guests arriving at the palace were greeted with a 120-foot high bronze statue of Nero, dressed as the sun god, on the porch.

His extravagance did not stop at the palace doors. Nero's public claim on Rome was unprecedented—preparing banquets in public places and treating

Nero's Torches, Henryk Siemiradzki, 1876, National Museum in Krakow, Poland

the city as a private party place. He "used the whole city, so to say, as his private house," writes Tacitus, who was a child during Nero's reign.

On one occasion, he had his guests towed on a barge around a lake in the Campus Martius; its banks lined with brothels and "naked prostitutes."

"These vessels glittered with gold and ivory," continues Tacitus, "Birds and beasts had been procured from remote countries, and sea monsters from the ocean…As darkness approached, all the adjacent grove and surrounding buildings resounded with song, and shone brilliantly with lights."

On Nero's death at the age of 31, his successors sought to wipe all traces of him from Rome. As the public breathed a sigh of relief that his campaign of terror was over, the Domus Aurea was largely destroyed, incorporated into new palaces or built over by public works such as the baths of Titus and Trajan.

Nero left behind a record of mind-boggling cruelty, but also a priceless legacy of ancient paintings and interior decoration, which would inspire artists across the centuries.

THE EXCAVATIONS OF THE DOMUS AUREA

The Finding of the Laocoön, by Hubert Robert, 1773

In the early 16th century, a treasure chest of art and antiquities was discovered by chance on the Oppian Hill, along the Via della Domus Aurea. In 1506, while digging in his vineyard on the Esquiline Hill, a grape grower fell upon an antique sculpture, depicting the sacrifice of a Trojan priest and his sons to sea serpents, which had adorned the Domus of Titus. The discovery of the famed marble *Laocoön*, now in the Vatican Museums, led in turn to that of several halls of Nero's Domus Aurea under the Oppio.

Within the chambers, lay a booty of large frescoes, painted and gilded stucco decoration, mosaic fragments and marble paneling. The discovery led to an art-rush, with Renaissance greats including Raphael, Pinturicchio, Giulio Romano and Giovanni da Udine heading to the Oppio to witness these wonders. Some of their signatures can still be seen gratified on the walls in graphite or carbon black pigment.

The ornamental grotesques of mythological creatures, and fantastic figures and animals, were a major reference point for this group as they decorated splendid residences for popes and cardinals. Today these inspirations of antiquity can be seen at the Vatican Palace, Castel Sant'Angelo, Villa Farnesina and Palazzo Barberini.

The paintings and stucco of the Domus Aurea, according to Rome's archeological office, are most likely by Fabullus, an artist noted by Pliny the Elder for his dramatic use of color—cinnabar, blue, dark red, indigo and green pigments—and penchant for painting in a toga. He may have had a "grave and serious personage," wrote the historian, having witnessed him at work, but he was a painter "in the florid style."

The first serious excavations of the Domus Aurea lasted a decade from 1758, and had continued off-and-on to this day. Dozens of rooms have been opened up, with others yet to be excavated or inaccessible.

CHAPTER 9

HADRIAN & ANTINOUS: DROWING AND DEIFICATION OF AN EMPEROR'S LOVER

130 A.D.

In A.D. 130, during an official visit to Egypt, Emperor Hadrian's beautiful young lover Antinous drowned in the Nile. No explanation was given at the time, though the emperor later insisted it was an accident. Rumors of Antinous being sacrificed, sacrificing himself or being murdered, ran riot. Hadrian became a laughing stock for his excessive mourning and idolization of Antinous. He mended his broken heart at his splendid country villa in Tivoli, where he died eight years after the mystery on the Nile.

Hadrian and Antinous, the "minion and slave of his unlawful pleasure," as St. Athanasius described him in his 4th-century writings, had been living together for several years before leaving together on an official trip to Egypt in 130 A.D., accompanied by Hadrian's wife Sabina. Worshipped by Hadrian—though not necessarily by all those in his imperial court— Antinous had just turned 18 at the time of his death, while the emperor was in his mid fifties.

Painting himself as tolerant and peaceful compared to brutal tyrants such as Nero, and initially admired for his moderation and building program, Hadrian became increasingly unpopular and isolated during his reign,

Hadrian and Antinous in the Palace at Lochias in Alexandria, by Otto Knille, 1832-1898

partly for a series of despotic executions.

Nevertheless he left an indelible stamp on the Roman Empire, drawing up new frontiers, including the famous Hadrian's Wall on the British-Scottish border, built to "separate the Romans and the barbarians."

At the time of Hadrian's reign, homosexuality was a common and acceptable practice, an attitude inherited from the Greeks. So strong was Hadrian's emulation of Hellenistic ways, he was nicknamed "Graeculus", the little Greek.

As Edward Gibbon noted wryly in his 1782 tome on the Roman Empire, "Yet we may remark, that of the first fifteen emperors, Claudius was the only one whose taste in love was entirely correct."

Having found the perfect Greek lover in Antinous, he incensed his courtiers with his excessive public displays of affection and pandering to his *inamorato*. A male lover was not meant by any means take the place of an "Augusta" (an Empress), yet Hadrian patently demonstrated more commitment to his male concubine than to his wife, and it was certainly Antinous he favored. Sabina and Hadrian put on a public face, despite the fact they apparently fought rabidly behind the scenes.

The emperor's love affair with Antinous ended in tragedy, when after embarking on a voyage up the Nile with the imperial entourage, Antinous apparently fell from the boat. His body was found floating in the river, near a small town called Besa. No truly plausible cause for the drowning was ever given. Superstition, conspiracies, and talk of cover-ups and sordid personal

Hadrian's Departure From The Villa At Tivoli, by
Eduardo Forti, 1880-1920

accusations have clouded the mystery even since ancient Rome historian Aelius Spartianus suggested Antinous died from "the beauty of Hadrian's sensuality."

Writing a century later, historian Cassius Dio pointed the finger at Hadrian and his dabbling in all kinds of "divinations and incantations." Rejecting the idea of Antinous tumbling by accident into the river, as Hadrian maintained in his autobiography, Dio figured the boy was "offered in sacrifice," or willingly surrendered his life to save that of the emperor.

Had the emperor consulted a soothsayer in Besa, been warned that danger was imminent, and that the sacrifice of someone near and dear was necessary in order for him to survive? Claims that Antinous's death occurred on the same day locals commemorate the drowning in the Nile of the Egyptian god Osiris only intensified the sacrifice theories.

Hadrian's absolute adoration of Antinous makes his involvement highly implausible. He had made it clear to his court, that if any ill ever came of his lover, the culprit would be "skinned alive."

Political motivation is more believable, with modern archaeologists pointing to Hadrian's own knights, who feared the emperor may line up Antinous to succeed him as emperor.

Following the drowning, the emperor had his young lover deified and built townships, temples and statues in his name. Festivals, sculptures and sacred icons of his lover spread throughout the Empire. In the city of Antinoupolis, built on the spot nearest to where Antinous had died, temples and a red granite statue of him in the likeness of Osiris were erected.

Back in Rome, Hadrian was ridiculed for weeping "like a woman", and for attributing the death to supernatural causes. That the emperor took more

Hadrian Visiting a Romano British Pottery, Lawrence Alma-Tadema, 1884, Stedelijk Museum, Amsterdam

than a passing interest in magic, horoscopes and occultism was no secret, but his claim that Antinous had been reincarnated as a star, which he had seen with his own eyes, overstepped the mark.

St. Athanasius judged both harshly. Antinous is described as "a wretch, sordid and loathsome instrument of his master's lust," while Hadrian's edict deifying him "testified to the world how entirely the emperor's unnatural passion survived the foul object of it," and immortalized his shame.

Remarkably, Hadrian and his wife continued their Egyptian journey not just for a few weeks, but five years. They tripped about visiting sites such as the Colossi of Memnon—two massive pharaoh sculptures, which are said to burst into strange sounds every dawn. The imperial couple took the singing colossuses as an indication that they had been looked kindly upon by the gods.

Such a diversion seems odd, but it pretty much clears Sabina of any suspicion. Though the prolonged public humiliation she had suffered with all his philandering would certainly appear a good motive, Hadrian was hardly going to accompany his wife on a sightseeing whirl if he felt she had done away with his beloved. The year after returning to Rome, in 135, she died—of natural causes.

An increasingly despondent Hadrian retreated to his summer Villa Adriana in Tivoli. Here he created a miniature Empire, assembling the finest replicas of Classical architecture and landscape design from Egypt, Greece and Rome. Spread over 300 acres on the slopes of the Tiburtine Hills, the villa had Greek theaters and temples, Latin and Greek libraries, an imperial palace, a naval theater, small and large bathing complexes, swimming pools and stadiums—all laid out within courtyards and colonnades. At its heart was the Golden Square, swept within alternating columns of white cipollino marble and dark Egyptian granite. Understandably, this was the most famous of the emperor's weekenders.

In the two decades it took to complete, the melancholic emperor turned his villa into a shrine to his young lover, filling it with portraits of Antinous, statues of him in Egyptian dress, and a massive burial tomb.

The poignant tale of the adolescent and the emperor is like another Romeo and Juliet in Italy, retold in films, books and opera. It is a story of romance, tragedy and intrigue—with a dash of sexual taboo—wrapped up in everlasting mystery.

VILLA MEDICI: STATUES IN THE GARDEN

Antinous's memory lives on among the Renaissance terraces and handsome fountain-filled grounds of the Villa Medici, which sweep in the Eternal City from the Pincio Hill. Built in 1540, the villa's ownership passed from the hands of the famous Florentine family to those of Napoleon in 1801. Its fern-festooned garden house or casina is packed with rarities from the sculpture collection of its former owner, the papal aspirant and lover of the antiquities, Cardinal Ferdinando de' Medici. Among the hundreds of bas-reliefs, cameos, plaster casts, statues, torsos and portrait sculptures is a bust of Antinous.

A great connoisseur of Classical art, Hadrian surrounded himself with sculpture at Villa Adriana. Among the figures uncovered there, some are now found in the Vatican Museums and Musei Capitolini, and further afield, at the Metropolitan Museum of Art in New York and the Louvre in Paris. Quite a store wound up at Villa Adriana's neighbor, the Villa d'Este, for when Cardinal Ippolito II d'Este began to construct his 16th-century residence, he organized further excavations at the Adriana, and ran off with the artworks he fancied down the street. The ruins of the Villa Adriana, 18 miles east of Rome, are listed by UNESCO.

CHAPTER 10

FUN AND GAMES AT THE THERMAE: CARACALLA'S ROMAN BATHS

216 A.D.

From 25 B.C., public baths were a democratic cornerstone of daily life in ancient Rome: emperors, nobles, plebs, prostitutes, slaves and athletes had bathing rights. Fed by the mighty aqueducts, these bathing complexes steadily evolved from simple sanitary structures into grandiose temples of leisure and pleasure. Successive emperors drummed up popularity by building increasingly lavish *thermae*, culminating in the opening of the Baths of Caracalla in 216 A.D. Eleven times the length of an Olympic swimming pool and accommodating 1600 bathers, Caracalla's Thermae Antoninianae were a monument to the megalomaniac Emperor Marcus Aurelius Antoninus, whose emulation of muscleman Hercules was on show at the baths.

Having killed his co-emperor brother Geta in a similar way that Romulus got Remus out of the picture, 26-year-old Caracalla got along with the job of absolute rule in 212 A.D.

Launching immediately into a self-aggrandizing construction boom, his baths at the foot of the Aventine Hill were to be bigger and better than all others. The tradition of democratic dipping began with Augustus, who on his

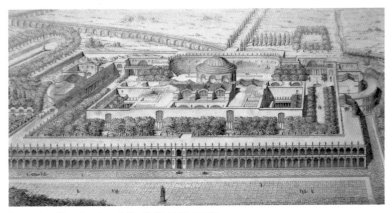

Reconstruction drawing of the Bath of Caracalla

death in 14 A.D. left the Thermae Agrippae to the Roman people "for their free use." Building the most elaborate and luxuriously decorated baths in a poor neighborhood was more than tradition for Caracalla—it was a publicity stunt.

While the upper class frequented private or more fashionable public baths in the Campus Martius and on Esquiline Hill, the Baths of Caracalla were built at a safe distance from the city center, and intended, it has been said, for the promiscuous plebs.

Caracalla lathered up huge public support, satisfying the people's growing demand for sensual pleasure; he also gained watery acquiescence and atonement, dazzling the mob and diverting public attention away from his atrocities.

After ordering his guards to murder Geta, who died in his mother's arms, Caracalla launched into a violent purge of 20,000 of his sibling's presumed supporters—or those who simply dared criticize the murder. Ferocious, paranoid and mentally unstable, he is rumored to have tried to kill his father, and had his wife Plautilla and her brother Plautius banished to the Aeolian island of Lipari, and later put to death, after their father, Plautianus, was caught conspiring against his son-in-law emperor.

"Caracalla was haunted by the recollection of his crimes and sought to get rid of his remorse by hunting, chariot-racing and gladiatorial shows," wrote the English sage Francis Bacon, in his 16th-century essays. "The rest of his reign was passed in the perpetration of insane atrocities."

The massive fun and games parlor, spreading over 30 acres, was a diversion for Caracalla and his subjects.

Reconstruction drawing of the central hall (*frigidarium*) of the Baths of Caracalla

Unlike previous baths where the prime concern was hygiene, this was a showy leisure land of glamorous thrills and sensory satisfaction, similar to a modern seaside resort. With just a small copper coin, almost anyone could buy into the Emperor's lavish lifestyle.

On top of the usual series of hot, tepid and icy rooms—*caldarium*, *tepidarium* and *frigidarium*—Caracalla's baths offered entertainment theaters, temples, exhibition halls, gymnasiums, swimming pools, sitting rooms, games areas and private bathing boxes. Sandwiched between porticos and pilasters, the recreational halls were decorated with statues, stucco and paintings, while the grounds swept through tree-shaded esplanades, playgrounds and fun fountains.

A complete novelty was the way the baths provided physical and mental workout to the mobs: they flexed their muscles in the Greek style training and wrestling rooms or palaestra, and their minds in the lecture halls, seminar rooms, and Greek and Latin libraries, whose concrete shelves can still be seen at Caracalla's ruins. As the Latin poet Juvenal said, *mens sana in corpore sano*—a healthy mind in a healthy body.

Caracalla

The bathing mega-structure was a muscleman complex in a double sense: the sporting and gladiatorial heroes flexing their biceps at the public from mosaic wall panels also paid homage to Caracalla, who recognized himself in every strongman.

Wandering about in a Gallic cloak—a Caracallus—and blonde wig, he claimed to be a reincarnation of Alexander the Great and imitated Hercules, who was a recurrent motif at the baths. Colossal statues of him and other heroes and gods lined the grand halls; one Hercules figure stood in the center of the *frigidarium*. (The so-called "athlete mosaics" are now found in the Vatican Museums along with the massive broken limbed *Belvedere Torso*, a fragment of Caracalla's Hercules statue, which inspired Michelangelo.)

As Rome's plebs flexed, dipped, drank and caressed at Caracalla, they were up to their necks in emperor-worship.

Not everyone was blind to Caracalla's misdoings. Within a year of the baths' completion, he was murdered by one of his soldiers, as he dismounted from his horse, while traveling from Edessa in Roman Mesopotamia towards the battlefields.

Though Diocletian would out-brag Caracalla in the size of his baths a few decades later, Caracalla's is the best preserved of the ancient baths and Rome's largest relic after the Colosseum.

When the decline of the Roman Empire began, in the 4th century A.D., Rome had 1.5 million people and 900 baths. The *thermae* had been absorbed into a pleasure-seeking society, and emperors won popularity by catering to the growing hedonism that was sapping the moral fiber of the Empire.

As the baths gained in popularity, Roman society slid into decadent depths, loosening up—not necessarily for the better—under the influence of the mandatory nudity.

With people increasingly obsessed with bodybuilding and beautiful self-image, their attentions were diverted away from more serious subjects such as waging war and empire-building.

Caracalla: AD 211, by Lawrence Alma-Tadema, 1902

Reading one anonymous Latin epitaph, one could easily think that a corrupt, decayed and sensuous end was inevitable for the Roman Empire—a consequence of Roman life as it was, and still is, devastatingly pleasurable.

Balnea, vina, Venus corrumpunt corpora nostra; sed vitam faciunt balnea, vina, Venus.

"Baths, wine and love corrupt our bodies, but baths, wines, and love are life."

CULTURE AT THE BATHS

Out of use since the 6th century, the Baths of Caracalla were a favorite dreaming spot for romantic writers and poets such as Goethe and Shelley. More recently, the grandiose ruins along the Via delle Terme di Caracalla have been used as a backdrop to films and concerts by the likes of the Three Tenors.

The 1990 concert at the Baths marked the first collaboration between superstar singers Plácido Domingo, José Carreras, and Luciano Pavarotti, from then on known as the Three Tenors. The live album sold over 10 million copies, and the Three Tenors continued to tour, becoming one of the most successful classical acts of all time.

CHAPTER 11

MACHOS & VIRGIN MARTYRS: AGNES OF ROME IN PIAZZA NAVONA

EARLY 4TH CENTURY

The bell-towered Church of Sant'Agnese in Agone on the western flank of Piazza Navona is dedicated to 13-year-old Agnes of Rome, the Roman Catholic patron saint of girls, martyred on the same spot in the early 4th century. Her crime was daring to reject a love-struck suitor in favor of a life devoted to chastity and Christianity.

The legend of beautiful young Agnes and her valiant defense of her chastity has been retold in the Christian Church for nearly two thousand years. In the century immediately following her death, St. Jerome wrote that the allure of St. Agnes had already won her worldwide veneration.

Weaned a Christian, this innocent yet principled maiden, he says, was as remarkable for her sweet nature as she was in physical beauty. In art and iconography long blonde hair flows about her robe-covered shoulders—she supposedly used those golden locks to protect herself from, rather than to attract attention.

Among her many potential suitors, was the son of the Roman prefect Sempronius. Asking for her hand in marriage, St. Agnes repelled all his advances. He then tried to woo her with riches—golden jewelry and priceless gems—but the saintly Agnes would not budge.

"Away from me tempter!" she exclaimed, according to Anna Jameson in her antiquarian work on saints and martyrs from 1863, adding that Agnes had made up her mind to betroth herself to another, "a lover who is greater and fairer than any earthly suitor."

Refusing to reveal the identity of her otherworldly beau, the pious young woman added that the rewards for her faith in the Lord promised to way outshine the jewels she was currently being offered.

To add insult to injury, wrote Jameson, Agnes evoked with ardor the religious ecstasy she had experienced during the liaison. "I have tasted of the milk and honey of his lips and the music of his divine voice has sounded in mine ears: he is so fair that the sun and moon are ravished by his beauty, and so mighty that the angels of heaven are his servants!"

Her suitor's youthful male pride was mortally injured. Consumed with jealousy, the boy fell violently ill. When a doctor diagnosed his condition as the result of unrequited love, Sempronius sought to pressure Agnes's parents to arrange for his son to marry their daughter. Not only was he unsuccessful, but their nosy neighbors informed the prefect that Agnes had betrothed herself to Jesus Christ.

Sempronius summonsed Agnes and smugly suggested that in light of her opposition to the idea of "an earthly husband," she should enter the service of Vesta, the goddess of the hearth, becoming one of the Vestal Virgins who kept a fire on the altar of the Temple of Vesta in the Roman Forum burning.

Agnes cut the prefect down to size with her gutsy reply, wrote Jameson.

"You think if having chosen not to listen to your juvenile son, I am going to lower myself by bowing and scraping to narcissistic, meaningless icons, or even worse, the demons who control them?"

Despite Sempronius's threats that Agnes would die a cruel, painful death, she refused to fold. In a sadistic bid to wear her down, Sempronius ordered

Martyrdom of St. Agnes, Vincent Masip, 1540s, Prado Museum

his soldiers to drag Agnes to a place of infamy and subject her to "the most degrading outrages."

The brothel where she was to be raped, and thus lose her sacred virginity, lay in the arcades of the Stadium of Domitian, a venue for Greek-style athletic competitions. The name of the arena's poorly lit arcades—*fornices*—was a moniker for brothel in ancient Rome, and led to the word fornicate.

Sending Agnes "under the arches," meant sending her to a brothel. After being stripped bare and left to rot amid the depravity, instead she found herself protected by a sacred aura, with onlookers falling at her feet, wanting to venerate rather than violate her.

During her captivity, Agnes had a vision of herself appearing before

The Death of St Agnes, Ercole Ferrata, 1660-64, Sant'Agnese in Agone

Christ, draped in chaste white garments, and the whorehouse filled with "miraculous sun." Deciding this was the perfect occasion to have his wicked way with her, the younger Sempronius made his advances, and was struck by blindness and convulsions. Overwhelmed by compassion, Agnes was able to save him with her amazing powers, and the boy made a miraculous recovery.

Witnessing Agnes's phenomenal healing ability, Sempronius began showing signs of religious conversion—though tempted to set her free, he ended up capitulating to the cries of "down with the witch" from the crowd.

Officials lit a fire and threw Agnes on top, with her proclaiming her Christian faith loudly and proudly all the way.

Having survived the brothel with her virginity intact, she now miraculously endured the fire unscathed. One of the executioners received his orders to finish her off with a sword, and Agnes died bathed in blood, her gaze focused unwaveringly towards heaven.

THE EVE OF ST. AGNES

The Eve of St Agnes, by John Everett Millais, 1863

St. Agnes is the patron saint of girls, and legend has it that virgins may see their future husbands in their dreams during the night of St. Agnes's Eve on January 20.

For the ritual to work, the young girl was to go to bed without supper, and undress completely before climbing into bed naked. Lying on her back, with her hands under the pillow, she would dream of her future husband, who would kiss and feast with her.

The legend is immortalized in the 42-stanza poem by English Romantic John Keats "The Eve of St. Agnes", written in 1819.

SAINT CECILIA

Saint Cecilia, by Guido Reni, 1606

The 3rd century also had its virgin martyr, Cecilia. Married at 16 to the future saint, Valerian, he respected her vow of chastity provided he could see Cecilia's guardian angel for himself. Valerian agreed to convert, and after his baptism, he found Cecilia talking to an angel and carrying two crowns of roses. Cecilia, Valerian and his brother Tiburtius set about giving alms and burying the bodies of martyred Christians—but soon, they all met the same fate. After Cecilia survived a boiling bath, a trembling executioner then botched her beheading. In the three days it took her to die, she continued her charity work and arranged for her house to become a place of worship. The earliest church built there, in 500 A.D., became the Basilica di Santa Cecilia in Trastevere in the Middle Ages. Located on the Piazza di Santa Cecilia, its half-domed apse features shimmering Baroque-era mosaics depicting her legend. Composer Charles Gounod's *St. Cecilia Mass*, and other hymns and anthems dedicated to the patron saint of music can be heard pealing out over Trastevere on November 22, St. Cecilia Day.

CHAPTER 12.

ARENAS OF DEATH: A MARTYR MONK AT THE COLOSSEUM

404 A.D.

Built as a colossal amphitheatre under the Flavian Emperors in the 1st century A.D., the Colosseum is a powerful reminder of ancient Romans' industrial genius—and their insatiable thirst for violence. God forbid any man stand in the way of their blood lust, even in the early years of Christian Rome. Telemachus was brave enough to try. He helped stop the Romans in their bloody tracks, but only by sacrificing himself.

When the monk Telemachus arrived in Rome in 404 A.D., he found himself in the midst of steamy public excitement and cries of "to the Colosseum!", as crowds flocked to the games. He had come to the city specifically to protest the outrageous brutality of the gladiatorial games, which had been a staple Roman entertainment for centuries.

Gladiatorial combat was the Roman equivalent of the wrestling competitions between Etruscan slaves—each fight ending with yet another burial. In the 6th century, St. Augustine—while busy converting the English to Christianity on behalf of Pope Gregory—recounted a friend's delight at the bloody games in his *Confessions*.

< *Naval Combat* (detail), by Ulpiano Checa, 1894

"As he saw the blood he gulped the brutality along with it; he did not turn away but fixed his gaze there and drank in the frenzy, not aware of what he was doing, reveling in the wicked contest and intoxicated on sanguinary pleasure."

The birth of the Colosseum as a mega-stadium for spectacle, sport and slaughter was the brainchild of Emperor Titus Flavius Vespasianus, and initially called the Flavian amphitheatre in his honor. The Flavian dynasty produced three rulers — Vespasian, and his sons Titus and Domitian — between 69 and 96 A.D.

In his *Lives of the Caesars*, Suetonius — who lived through the Flavian reigns as a child and young adult — wrote that the trio brought stability and good government to Rome, after the chaos and carnage of Nero's reign. Stocky and fit, Vespasian was affable and witty, lenient and unassuming, but stingy — even Suetonius jokes, at his own funeral. Imitated at the internment by a mimic actor wearing a mask, Vespasian asks how much the service will cost. On hearing the reply "Ten million sesterces," the emperor cried out, "Give me a hundred thousand and fling me even into the Tiber."

Vespasian showed no such penny-pinching with the Colosseum. He built his amphitheater — the largest such arena in the Roman world — on land that was once part of Nero's opulent estate, the Domus Aurea.

The spherical mass of enormous travertine blocks was funded with the booty from Rome's siege of Jerusalem in 70 A.D., when the city was captured and destroyed. Finishing off the work he had begun with his father, Titus succeeded in quelling the revolt of Jews against Roman rule in Judea after four years of warring.

When the theater was finally completed by Titus in 80 A.D., the gory spectacle grew to astronomic proportions. The historian Cassius Dio recalled the lavish displays of violence at the theater: "One contest pitted whooping cranes against each other; in another four elephants fought. Animals both tame and wild were slaughtered, to the number of 9,000."

Spectacles at the Colosseum and other arenas lasted 100 days, and Titus was an exceptional stage manager and performer, Dio wrote. "He threw little

Pollice Verso, by Jean-Léon Gérôme, 1872, Phoenix Art Museum

wooden balls down on the audience of the amphitheatre, each inscribed with a little picture of the prize, that those who caught the balls could pick up from the appropriate officials: the prizes included food, clothing, vessels of silver and gold, horses, mules, cattle and slaves."

Titus "who did little that was exceptional," in Dio's estimation, aside from organizing these shows, was seen weeping at the close of one series of games.

In the crowded capital, the Colosseum was guaranteed capacity crowds. Not only was there free entry for all, Rome's population in the 2nd century had reached one million—a number unmatched until London in 1800.

Exotic creatures were imported from all over the Empire, and over 5,000 people and 11,000 animals slaughtered in one single series of games. In a single seating, some 80,000 Romans crammed into this arena of death, where special effects included flooding for mock sea battles. After filling the stadium with water, Titus brought in horses, bulls and other animals that had been trained for water tactics.

Though there is doubt over how watertight the Colosseum really was, according to Dio ships floated within its walls, laden with gladiators dressed to impersonate soldiers from the 433 B.C. Battle of Sybota.

For Romans, size mattered. The monumental scale of the Colosseum was an important symbol of the Empire's prosperity and potency. Behind its heavy exterior of superimposed arches and semi-circular columns lay a lavish interior of gold cladding, ivory and precious stone mosaics.

Some emperors used it more than others as a showground for their colossal egos. In 180 A.D., Lucius Aurelius Commodus spent lavishly on gladiatorial combats, and fancied a fight himself.

Commodus's arrival in power marked the end of the so-called reign of the Five Good Emperors: Nerva, Trajan, Hadrian, Antoninus Pius and Marcus Aurelius, Commodus's father.

Commodus was a lunatic who, considering himself both a god and Rome's second founder, renamed the city Colonia Commodiana. His mother, the Empress Faustina, was apparently as taken with gladiators as she was with senators and sailors, and gossips claimed Commodus was the son of a gladiator.

In a flurry of self-idolization, he erected statues of himself in Herculean poses about town, and appeared at the Colosseum, wrote Dio, "with all the trappings of Mercury," including golden winged sandals and staff, his shoulders draped in the purple cloth of royalty.

Unbothered by the ridicule he attracted for performing in the arena like a slave, Commodus, in his first gladiatorial contest, killed a hundred bears, gulping down "sweet wine" to sustain himself. Exotic animals including elephants, rhinoceros and giraffes were slaughtered in another two-day event. Fighting terms were hardly fair; his gladiator opponents were always armed with child's play weapons such as blunted batons.

At another show, he killed an ostrich and paraded its severed head and the bloody sword menacingly before his statesmen, grinning wickedly and insinuating he could do the same with them. Dio, who was also a politician,

The Emperor Commodus Leaving the Colosseum at the Head of the Gladiators, by Edwin Blashfield, 1878, Hermitage Museum & Gardens, Norfolk, Virginia

wrote that he and the other senators had to chew on the laurel leaves of their garlands to hide the fact they were laughing.

Commodus came to a violent end in 192, though not in his Colosseum. He was poisoned then strangled at the instigation of Marcia, his mistress, and his chief chamberlain and Praetorian Guard, after they learned they were next on the emperor's hit list.

When Telemachus arrived in 404, the games had been going on uninterrupted for centuries, even with Constantine's official recognition of Christianity during his emperorship from 312 A.D. Though Constantine was critical of the games, condemning the "art and amusement of shedding human blood" in his landmark edict, he did not impose an absolute ban.

Telemachus took more decisive action. Once inside the arena, he stood up bravely and bellowed for an end to the violence, before throwing himself into the circus. For his efforts to prick the public conscience the crowd ripped him to pieces, but his martyrdom was not entirely wasted. Emperor Honorius had closed down the gladiatorial schools in 399, but the fights continued. Upon the monk's death, the emperor delivered an edict for the games to end, and though it was not fully respected, the bloodbaths gradually subsided, before grinding to a complete halt the following century.

CHAPTER 13.

MAROZIA AND THEODORA: HARLOT RULE AT THE LATERAN PALACE

928

The dominating influence of noble courtesans over the papal court in the early part of the 10th century was so pervasive, a special term was coined to describe it: the *pornocracy*. Mother Theodora, and her daughters Marozia and Theodora II, changed the course of history, vanquishing their pontiff-lovers with their promiscuous powers to rule over the city and the papacy. Marozia out-maneuvered them all—the "she pope" was among other things, mistress, mother and assumed murderer of popes.

In 928, Pope John X, who had reigned for a remarkable thirteen years in an age of extreme papal-precariousness, died in a dungeon at the Castel Sant'Angelo. Most say he died from being smothered by a pillow, others from grief, after being arrested on Marozia's orders, stripped bare of all papal authority and thrown in prison.

In Marozia's days, power over popes was a family affair. Her mother, Theodora, had instigated John X's election in 914, relying on her beauty and talent to dominate church and state affairs. Marozia was a product of the same corrupt society, in which contending patrician families corroded the pope's governing or "temporal" powers, and gained the upper hand

View of the Piazza di San Giovanni in Laterano, by Bernardo Bellotto, c. 1744

on Roman political affairs. The placement of popes was crucial to the aristocracy's ability to gain and retain power.

All popes of this era were cherry-picked by a powerful aristocracy, who sought to advance their interests all the way to the Lateran Palace. For about three decades, the era of patrician rule became one of harlot rule, in which the affairs of the church and those of flesh were thickly enmeshed.

Not only was the papacy being unduly swayed by aristocratic influence during the *pornocracy*—the Lateran Palace, the papal residence until the 15th century, fell under the spell of noble courtesans, who were sneaking in and out of its bedchambers by night.

Marozia disliked her mother's beau, John X, and felt threatened by him. With him out of the way, she secured the elevation of her current pet pope, Leo VI. Gradually, she was maneuvering to see the pontifical throne occupied by her "own bastard son," the future Pope John XI—supposedly a fruit of her torrid teenage affair with Pope Sergius III.

Voltaire wrote about the episode and "all powerful" Marozia in one of his 18th-century essays: "This very Marozia conspired against the pope, who had been for so long a time her sister's gallant: upon which he was seized and smothered between two mattresses."

The Frenchman suggests Pope John X was the lover of Marozia's sister, Theodora II; he was definitely the lover of their mother, Theodora, and may well have been one of Marozia's papal playthings as well.

When Emperor Constantine the Great gave Christians the green light for freedom of religious worship in his 313 edict, he paved the way for the gradual rise of church leadership of the state. The Roman church wasted no time doting

Marozia, Senatrix of Rome,

itself with a sophisticated internal organization, which laid the foundations for its growth, and international expansion.

When a series of barbarian invasions beset the Western Roman Empire from the 3rd century onwards, the imperial government's efforts were focused elsewhere—on its eastern interests in the Byzantine Empire. The popes were left to fill in the gap, and gradually replaced the emperors, to rule over Rome as monarchs. By the 5th century, the papacy was proclaiming itself to be the source of all Christianity.

The far-flung Lateran district in southeast Rome, blossomed together with Christianity in the 5th century; an arm's length from the still pagan ruling classes, its isolation much later threatened to curb the power of the church. In the 9th and 10th centuries, location was really the least of the worries for the morally and politically impoverished papacy.

The so-called *pornocracy* began with the election of Pope Sergius III in 904; restoring the Lateran following an earthquake was the only positive aspect of his licentious office. Morals were loose at the Lateran under the lusty pope; even former nuns did not stop short at describing it as a "whorehouse".

"The papal palace became a vast seraglio; the very churches echoed to

Pope John XI

obscene songs and bacchanal festivities," wrote Alfred Owen Legge in his 1870 book, *The Growth of the Temporal Power of the Papacy*.

For about three decades, the terrible trio—Theodora and her daughters—pulled the strings on their puppet popes; behind them was the family's patriarch Theophylact, a Roman consul of noble descent, whose wife and daughters simply extended his desire for power to the bedroom.

As a team, they performed incredible legwork to see their favorites, often disreputable men with absolutely no connection to the church, fill the papal chair.

The papal tiara often ended up on the head of the "most strenuous of their lovers," jibed 18th-century British historian Edward Gibbon, noting that "the influence of two sister prostitutes" was "founded on their wealth and beauty". Once their man was in office, the concubines of the clergy continued to usurp powers, by spinning viperous webs of political and personal intrigue. It was the closest Rome had ever come to having a "female pope."

Liutprand of Cremorna, a contemporary of the depraved Marozia, wrote about her relationship with Sergius III, and the manner in which Theodora shared powers, and popes, with her daughter. As for Marozia, he labeled her a reckless whore, who ruled over Rome like a man.

Nonetheless, Marozia outperformed her mother as a "mistress of Rome." She was a propagator of popes—mother, grandmother and great-grandmother—and succeeded in navigating her lineage into the seat of St. Peter's. The volatile era, which she and her progeny presided over for the first half of the 10th century, is described as the dark ages of the papacy—*Saeculum obscurum*.

During this lustful period, the standard reign for popes was often no more than a year; some luckier pontiffs beat the odds to last a few years, even a decade, only to be deposed, imprisoned or dealt a violent death. A sudden shifting of allegiances, stormy lover's row or switching of bed partners at the Lateran could have dramatic consequences.

Pope John XII

The tables would eventually turn on 44-year-old Marozia, for she had spawned not only popes, but a viperous, backstabbing and power-grabbing matrix. Shortly after seeing her son John XI elected pope in 931, another son (from her first marriage), Alberic II, led a revolt against Marozia, ostensibly to bring to an end his mother's tyranny.

Alberic stormed the Castel Sant'Angelo, where Marozia was ensconced, and had his mother, her third husband and the pope imprisoned. His half-brother was kept under house arrest at the Lateran until his death, and while the circumstances are shadowy surrounding Marozia's fate, it is most likely that she was locked up in a convent.

Like mother, like son. Assuming the title of "Prince and Senator of the Romans," Alberic ruled Rome until his death in 954, during which time he appointed four popes.

Before he died, Alberic ordered the Papal Curia and his aristocrat chums swear an oath, that his illegitimate son, Octavian—Marozia's grandson—would be the next pope. His wish was met: Octavian became Pope John XII at 18, his 11-year office as profligate and debauched as the rest.

Even though a man was now picking the popes, the *pornocracy* still had a grip. After all, it was Marozia's son who was now in bed with the popes—at least politically.

CHAPTER 14.

MURDER ON CAPITOLINE HILL: COLA DI RIENZO, REFORMIST HERO TURNED TYRANT

1354

Amid the rife political anarchy and corruption of the Middle Ages, lawyer and scholar Cola di Rienzo championed a populist movement to revive the golden days of the Roman Republic and rid Rome of its ruling patricians. He lost the plot, transforming from an orating visionary into a vainglorious sovereign on Capitoline Hill—Campidoglio—the same place where he lost his life.

In the 14th century, Rome was caught in a political vacuum. The papacy had moved camp to Avignon in France, pressed by French king Philip IV, who played a deciding role in the 1305 election of Pope Clement V.

Rome was left at the mercy of the controlling, covetous and unstable rule of local families. The void was filled by the cancerous influence of powerful, warring factions among the Roman elite—the pro-papal Orsini and emperor-supporting Colonna families. The situation preoccupied young notary Cola di Rienzo—Nicola, the son of Lorenzo, an innkeeper in Trastevere.

After his mother died, Cola spent his youth with relatives in the countryside near Rome, nourishing himself, wrote Edward Gibbon in his classic history

---

‹ *Statue of Cola Di Rienzo* (front), by Girolamo Masini, 1877, erected on the slope of the Campidoglio where he was killed

91

of Rome, on the ancient classics and studying "with indefatigable diligence the manuscripts and marbles of antiquity."

Emulating the great Latin poets and orators, his eloquence and rhetorical skills won him respect in civic circles, as well as diplomatic assignments from public authorities.

In 1343, at the age of 30, he was sent on a mission to Avignon to beseech Clement VI for a return of the papacy to Rome.

The impressed pope appointed him as notary to the Camera Urbis, the Roman civic chamber on Capitoline Hill, allowing him to write and speechify to his heart's content while supervising income and taxes. Addressing the mob on the Capitoline, the self-styled tribune cleverly presented himself as a mouthpiece of the oppressed, promising them an end to the aristocratic milking of the coffers and official reckoning for the host of unpunished murders and rapes committed by the nobility.

His thirst for ridding Rome of its outlaw barons and restoring justice escalated when his young brother was slain in a skirmish between the two warring families.

On May 20, 1347, with public protection and a church nod, Rienzo began his revolution against the ruling elite, with strong support from the mob. In full armor, he marched to Capitoline Hill and proclaimed the return of the ancient Roman Republic. As church bells pealed over the Tiber, the aristocrats were forced out of the senatorial palace and of the city, and the pope nominated Cola "Rector of Rome."

Cola had initial success establishing law, order and accountability; as he penned political theory, his ideas resonated with the foreign dignitaries and philosophers with whom he corresponded. One of his great admirers was the humanist and poet Francesco Petrarch, who hankered equally for a return to the "old order."

Once he was in a position of power, Cola lost sight of his role as popular political reformer. Though eloquent and erudite, he was no statesman, but foisted himself off as one in the most inflated fashion. Out of his depth

Rienzi Vowing to Obtain Justice for the Death of his Young Brother, Slain in a Skirmish between the Colonna and the Orsini Factions, by William Holman Hunt, 1849

as a leader, he let the authority go to his head, and stepped way beyond his mandate.

In a flash, he switched from dissenter to oppressor, a neo-emperor, cushioning himself and his family members in a life of luxury and privilege, paid for by mounting taxes and stolen public and church money.

His initial self-proclaimed role as "tribune of the people" developed into a string of bombastic titles: Candidate of the Holy Spirit (*Candidatus Spiritus Sancti*), Liberator of the City (*Liberator Urbis*), Defender of Italy (*Zelator Italic*), and Emperor of the World (*Imperator Orbis*), to name but a few.

Posing as a sovereign with a crown, specter and fur-lined satin gown, he held extravagant processions and banquets. On public parades, he rode on a white steed, with the Republican banner—a sun with a circle of stars and dove with olive branch—flying overhead. Gold and silver coins were showered in his trail, among the crowds. At one dinner, buffoons dressed up in bull skins and horns leapt about entertaining guests. The final straw came, in August 1347, when he rode on horseback through the streets to the Basilica di San Giovanni in Laterano, triumphantly escorted by trumpet-blowing guards.

Dressed in a purple coat, and swords and spurs, he bathed in the baptistery of S. Giovanni in Fonte—which had supposedly cured Constantine of leprosy—before crowning himself emperor.

Cola di Rienzo Haranguing the Crowd, by Dario Querci, 1871, Museo di Roma

With Rienzo denounced in a papal bull as a criminal and heretic, by December 1347, Rome was back in the hands of the ruling nobles, and he was on the run. After holing up in the Castel Sant'Angelo, he left the city and spent several years wandering, sheltered by Franciscan monks or in prison.

Astoundingly, he got a second shot at putting Rome right. In August 1354, after two years under papal custody in Avignon, Pope Innocent IV sent Rienzo back to Rome, to restore the crumbled papal authority. Some say Innocent was won over by Rienzo's do-gooder spiel, others that his motive was one of deliberate mischief making, in putting the cat back among the pigeons.

The political anarchy in Rome was sufficiently dire for his crimes to have been purged from public memory. The crowds gave him a hero's return, reinstating his former diktats and again driving the nobles out. His comeback was short lived. Hedonism, dictatorial killings and more raiding of the papal and public purses were hallmarks of his four-month reign.

Some historians suggest his classical education may have led to his downfall. The great knowledge Rienzo had acquired, for as much as it was a virtue, also corrupted him, wrote Gibbon, for it was "tinctured with the adjacent vices; justice with cruelty, liberality with profusion, and the desire of fame with puerile and ostentatious vanity."

On October 8, 1354, the cry of "Death to Rienzo the traitor!" rose over Capitoline Hill. As Rienzo addressed the crowd from the balcony of the Senators' Palace, dressed in protective helmet and armor, a volley of stones and insults were hurled his way.

After being struck in the hand by an arrow, Rienzo attempted to flee, camouflaged in a monk's habit, but he was spotted and seized by the angry mob. Fed up with his turncoat behavior, his captors stabbed him repeatedly at the foot of the Capitoline stairs, right alongside two white lions carved from Egyptian porphyry. They then dragged his corpse through the streets, cut of his head and hung his body by the feet from a balcony in the Piazza San Marcello, near the Colonna Palace.

PIAZZA DEL CAMPIDOGLIO

From the Piazza d'Araceoli, at the base of the Capitoline, two parallel staircases ascend the hill. Standing in great contrast, one is a crumbling old stairway to the sky—the other a gleaming Renaissance appurtenance.

In Rienzo's times, a long near step-less ramp, or *cordonata*, led from the medieval city to the hilltop Palazzo Senatorio, the town hall on the Piazza del Campidoglio. He replaced that with the acutely steep stairway, the Scalinata dell'Aracoeli, in 1348—its 124 marble steps lead to the Santa Maria in Aracoeli church. The stairs were one of the tribune's favorite haranguing points.

Starting in 1537, Michelangelo gave the precinct a makeover, adding his very own *cordonata*—the stairway that unfurls like a broad streamer towards the hilltop Piazza del Campidoglio, in giant-sized strides. On the way up, you will pass by a bronze statue of Cola di Rienzo in his hooded cloak, in the grassy strip between the Aracoeli staircase and Michelangelo's *campidgolio* staircase—the place where fate caught up with him.

CHAPTER 15.

REBUILDING ROME: FROM URBAN DISASTERS TO MIRACLES

1450

In 1450, scores of Christian pilgrims died when panic erupted on the narrow Ponte Sant'Angelo leading to St. Peter's Basilica. The Jubilee year, planned for so carefully by Pope Nicholas V, culminated in calamity. Ten centuries after Constantine opened the floodgates to Christianity, Rome was unfit for pilgrim masses. The tragedy prompted sweeping renewal of Rome's urban architecture—spurred on by massive papal patronage, a big chunk of ancient treasures was recovered and enriched. The *renovatio urbis* shored up pontifical power, while gearing the city up for the artistic glory of the Renaissance.

What started as a trickle in the 5th century of primarily wandering monks had developed into a small flood of cross-continental pilgrims by the 12th century. Rome was one of the major destinations for medieval pilgrimage, and the numbers of those coming to see the city's holy sites peaked in Jubilee or Holy Years.

Far from a romantic trip, pilgrimage was packed with perils, and travelers generally drew up their will before setting out. After health and hijacking threats mid-journey, once in Rome, pilgrims faced headaches securing bed

Pons Aelius, 1762

and board, unruly crowds and dodgy buildings. The city was ill equipped to deal with large influxes, and many antiquities the crowds had come to see were on the verge of collapse.

From his ascension in 1447, the Florentine Pope, Nicholas V, set about changing all that. Following on the heels of Eugenius IV, who focused on furthering Rome's international rank as a spiritual power, Nicholas V turned his focus to the city's crumbling architecture, determined to restore its glory in time for his Jubilee in 1450.

Widely known as the "first Renaissance pope," Nicholas V (born Tommaso Parentucelli) brought humanist ideals to Rome, and an ambitious program to rebuild the city, which was groaning under the weight of age and over-crowdedness. The first pope to sponsor Rome's renovation, his *renovatio urbis* led to refortification of the Castel Sant'Angelo, facelifts for the Palazzo Senatorio and other municipal buildings on Capitoline Hill, and repairs to city walls and churches.

He also made the major decision to shift the papal residence from the run-down Lateran Palace to the Vatican, where he added new wings and planned a radical reconstruction of St. Peter's.

Some changes did not come soon enough. Congestion in the city crescendoed during the 1450 Holy Year celebrations. Thousands of pilgrims had swarmed to get a glimpse of "Veronica's veil"—a small cloth imprinted with the *Volto Santo*, the Holy Image, which St. Veronica supposedly used to wipe Jesus's face on his way to his crucifixion at Calvary.

The Ponte Sant'Angelo led them to St. Peter's—the bridge was built by Emperor Hadrian in 134 A.D. to link up his family mausoleum with the city-side of the Tiber. The narrow medieval streets leading to the bridge were jam packed with pilgrims. As crowds clamored around the rosary sellers on the bridge, panic broke out and one of the parapets collapsed. Two hundred pilgrims died, either drowning or being trampled in the throng, leaving the public and church leaders in shock.

After the disaster, Pope Nicholas V got rid of the rosary shops, which were impeding pedestrian flow, and improved access to the bridge. It would be another two centuries before Bernini's angels beautified it, but things were already pointing strongly in that direction.

The Veil of Veronica, by Domenico Fetti, c. 1620, National Gallery of Art, Washington, D.C.

The unprecedented architectural renewal of Rome's crumbling relics accompanied an era of papal resurgence—and artistic riches were soon to play a part in the equation. The popes of the 15th century sought to wed Rome's image as a Holy Metropolis with the authority of the church. If buildings were to be political statements, they had to make them crowd-proof to avoid repetition of the Ponte Sant'Angelo incident.

What greater symbol for propagating papal power than St. Peter's.

Built by Constantine in the 4th century, the basilica had steadily fallen into disrepair. According to Nicolas V's chief architect, Leon Battista Alberti, collapse was imminent.

As a team, the two Florentines geared Rome up for Renaissance splendor, restoring past glories, and building new ones. Alberti's *Descriptio urbis Romae* (Delineation of the City of Rome) prescribed a precise rebuilding of Rome and revival of its ancient monuments from the Colosseum to the Arch of Constantine. According to one of Alberti's biographers, "No one did more to call the lost city of the ancients back to life."

To ready the city for the pilgrim masses, Nicholas V wanted to enlarge St. Peter's and add a grand public square for papal blessings, but he did not live long enough to see this completed.

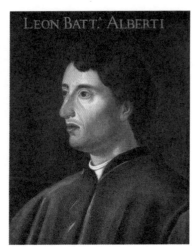

Left: *Pope Nicolas V*, by Peter Paul Rubens, 1612-16; right: *Leon Battista Alberti*

His successors completed many of his unfinished ideas, notably at the Vatican and St. Peter's, and improved city infrastructure to ensure safe and efficient access to the Vatican area.

The Sistine Chapel's namesake, Sixtus IV, prepared frenetically for the Holy Year in 1475, restoring dozens of churches, and fortifying bridges and aqueducts. A new road, the Via Sistina, facilitated access to the Ponte Sant'Angelo, while the Ponte Sisto bridge created a new "Vatican way," linking the city center to Trastevere.

The crown jewel of his achievements was the Botticelli-decked Sistine Chapel inaugurated in 1483. Sandro Boticelli was one of several noted Florentine painters Sixtus brought to Rome to work on the chapel's frescos, wanting them finished quickly but masterfully. Biblical stories from the life of Moses adorn the left wall—stories from the life of Christ the right wall.

Even the dark themes in Botticelli's gold-leaf glittering *Punishment of Korah* bear out the magnificence of the new papal chapel.

Six decades of urban restoration and enrichment in Rome culminated under Julius II della Rovere, who radically transformed the small city between

1503 and 1513. He inaugurated the rebuilding of St. Peter's, summonsing the art superstars of the epoch, Raphael and Michelangelo to help him achieve his aims. As Raphael worked on the pope's private apartments (the four rooms now referred to as the Stanze di Raffaello), Michelangelo began the first of his two long stints in the Sistine Chapel, starting with the hallowed ceiling.

These two popes continued to draw on the blueprint of Nicholas V — a great builder and humanist. In his dying breaths, he spelled out the philosophical pedestal of his architectural program: The "majestic monuments" were not inspired by personal ambition and vanity, but "to create solid and stable convictions in the minds of the uncultured masses."

Religious doctrine was flimsy, Nicolò believed, unless underpinned by a tangible learning experience. Cultivating public faith, required emotional nourishment — true believers needed to behold true beauty.

In the pilgrim-ready city of today, with its remarkable interwoven layers of antique, Baroque and Renaissance splendor, his words ring out as loud as the bells of St. Peter's.

CHAPTER 16

LUCREZIA BORGIA: VILLAINESS OR VICTIM AT THE VATICAN PALACE

1500

Lucrezia Borgia was born on April 18, 1480, into the most scandalous Renaissance family to rule Rome from the Vatican. She was the last of Cardinal Rodrigo Borgia's illegitimate children, and within a year of his coronation as Pope Alexander VI, in 1492, he married the 13-year-old off to further his political goals. Raised in a most unholy household, with a nepotistic, scheming, fornicating father, and lusty, ruthless brother as role models, the blue-eyed, blond-haired beauty has been cast throughout history as a Vatican villainess. In truth, she was more likely a political pawn for the house of Borgia and a victim of bad press.

In his 1867 book on the Italian Renaissance, the French Count Arthur Gobineau describes "an audacious scene" unfolding at the Borgia apartments at the Vatican. Pope Alexander VI is in the throws of defending his son, Cesare Borgia, who has just strangled his brother-in-law, Alfonso of Aragon. Cesare's sister, Lucrezia, is standing by witnessing the brutal murder of her husband by her spiteful brother.

"He is not a monster, my daughter, but a ruler who could not enter his destined sphere but at the price of the most sustained and sometimes the

---

Disputation of St. Catherine, by Pinturicchio, 1492, Borgia Apartments, Vatican Museums. The figure of St. Catherine was modeled on Lucrezia.

most pitiless effort," the pope explains to Lucrezia in Gobineau's account.

"No, Holy Father," the girl replies. "I am nothing but a wretched woman whose family makes her a mere pawn in the game, whose interests are no more considered than her feelings."

Murders, cruelty, corruption, orgies, political plots, poisonings, astronomical wealth, greed and ambition—the Borgias brought to the Vatican corridors every possible ingredient for sensational storytelling. What stands out is the ambiguous portrayal of Lucrezia, cast as either a notorious femme fatale or the complete opposite, a saint.

From a tender age, she had been educated in the mechanics of depravity, watching her father bribe and flatter his way to the Vatican's top job, and witnessing his antics as a papal playboy. Dripping in wealth from his bishoprics and titles, Borgia, a charismatic and cultured lover of Bacchanalian orgies, was ruled by insatiable sensuality.

Lucrezia's mother, Vannozza dei Cattanei, was the cardinal's long-term mistress. He had four children with her, including Cesare and Lucrezia.

Portrait of Gentleman, aka Cesare Borgia, by Altobello Melone, 1500-24, Galleria dell'Accademia Carrara, Italy

When Rodrigo tired of Vannozza, he took up with 15-year-old Giulia Farnese, the "pope's whore," as she quickly came to be known. Forty-three years his junior and already married, the extraordinarily beautiful but calculating "Giulia la Bella" became another role model for Lucrezia. The Borgia Pope possibly pressured Farnese's husband, Orsino Orsini, to go and live in his castle in northern Italy, in order to have Giulia— "Christ's bride," as she was also caustically referred to—all to himself.

Once at the Vatican, Borgia plotted his children's destinies with the same cunning that brought him there: conferring the lucrative bishopric of Valencia on Cesare, and organizing Lucrezia's marriage to the powerful Giovanni Sforza, the Lord of Pesaro. Promoting his children's fortunes was one of Borgia's main goals. Powerful, irascible and riddled with contradictions, he loved his children intensely, but largely mistook his own interests for theirs.

Lucrezia was helplessly trapped in his dynastic dreams. While still a cardinal, he paired her up with rich Spanish suitors, but the marriage contracts were just as quickly annulled, according to his own whims and fancies, and when a better offer came by.

In 1497, 17-year-old Lucrezia's marriage to Sforza was annulled on the grounds of impotency. Within a year, she had remarried, this time to Alfonso of Aragon—the 19-year-old Duke of Bisceglie—who was murdered in the Borgia's Vatican quarters in 1500.

Johannes Burchard, Alsatian-born priest and papal master of ceremonies, recorded the circumstances of the attack in his *Diarium*—a journal of his time at the court of the Borgias.

Copy of destroyed Pinturicchio fresco. *"Pope Alexander VI before Madonna* (his favorite Giulia Farnese)," as decribed by Vasari. Made by Pietro Facettio, 16th century

Alfonso was assailed by a group of knife-wielding assassins who left him for dead, Burchard wrote. They fled the city, via the Pertusa Gate (in the Medieval city walls), with the help of some forty horsemen. The dying prince was taken to a chamber of the Borgia Tower, where a cardinal gave him the papal blessing, *in articulo mortis*, on the point of death.

Two days later, Alfonso died, a surprise to many, as after close medical attention, he was thought to be out of danger.

"Not dying from the wound he had taken," wrote Burchard, "he was yesterday strangled in his bed at the nineteenth hour."

The notoriously crafty Cesare—caricatured in Niccolò Machiavelli's 1513 manual of political manipulation, *The Prince*—was implicated, just as he was in the murder of his brother Giovanni, Duke of Gandia, whose body was netted out of the Tiber on June 14, 1497—stabbed over a dozen times with a slender stiletto dagger, his throat had been slashed, hands tied and a stone hung 'round his neck.

Pens and rumors have run riot on the Borgia tale, making it more lurid than reality.

Some of the vicious stories about Lucrezia arose from gossip—rumors of incest with her father and brother were fanned by an insulted Giovanni Sforza when forced to officially admit his impotency.

A Glass of Wine with Caesar Borgia, by John Collier, 1893, Ipswich Museum and Art Gallery, UK

In the moral wasteland of Renaissance Rome, where there was no differentiating church saints from town harlots, the Borgias held the stage. All the children, like their father, were consumed with a desire for power.

In the papal apartments, Lucrezia grew up amid imagery of angels, clutching in their uplifted hands the Borgia heraldry adorned with the three-tiered papal tiara and keys to the kingdom of heaven. Though she was certainly no angel, unlike her father, Lucrezia did not blaze a sinner's trail to the most powerful church position in the world.

She may have been an innocent bystander on much of the Borgias' wicked ways, but Lucrezia was no wallflower when it came to their hedonistic partying. In his diaries, Burchard described one outrageous banquet held in the 190-foot long Sala Reale (the great hall) of the papal palace, when fifty courtesans danced naked between ballet performances, watched over by the

Portrait thought to be of *Lucrezia Borgia*, artist unknown

Pope, Cesare and 21-year-old Lucrezia.

"Following the supper, lampstands holding lighted candles were placed on the floor and chestnuts strewn about, which the prostitutes—naked on the floor, on their hands and knees—had to pick up, as they crawled in and out amongst the lampstands …Prizes were offered—silken doublets, pairs of shoes, hats and other garments—for those men who were most successful with the prostitutes."

A paradigm of virtue perhaps not, but Lucrezia may well have stayed in her marriage to Alfonso of Aragon (albeit with all kinds of sensory indulgences elsewhere), if it had not been for her family. The opportunity to escape their grip presented itself, after two doomed marriages, when she married Alfonso d'Este, the Duke of Ferrara, in 1501.

As Duchess of Ferrara, she mothered five children, and transformed the court into a center of culture by patronizing painters Titian and Dosso Dossi, and poet Pietro Bembo.

She took the latter, a cardinal, as her lover, and their 18-year romance was sweetened by numerous love letters.

Lucrezia also maintained a secret, lifelong liaison with her brother-in-law, Francesco Gonzaga—husband of Alfonso d'Este's sister.

From 1508 to 1512, she was not only a doting patron and mother, but *de facto* ruler of Ferrara, during her husband's frequent absence.

Lucrezia's strong-minded nature blossomed when she was queen of her own castle, and no longer condemned to be a casualty of her family's poisonous chess moves. In Ferrara, she managed business, home and love affairs with great dexterity and ambition.

Her shrewdness was tempered by abiding kindness and forgiveness—she looked out for her father and brother for the rest of their lives.

For over a decade, leading up to her death in 1519, Lucrezia was almost constantly pregnant. Weakened by several miscarriages and the death of a newborn, the duchess died during childbirth at the age of 39—not long after her husband had returned to be by her side.

CHAPTER 17.

MICHELANGELO: TORMENT OF THE SISTINE CHAPEL
1508—1512

Between 1508 and 1512, young Florentine artist Michelangelo Buonarroti labored around-the-clock on the ceiling of the Vatican Palace chapel. The physical fallout from this and his subsequent stint at the Sistine as a 60-year-old was horrendous, as witty poems and woeful letters to friends and family reveal—not to mention his medical record.

As he painted the Sistine, 33-year-old Michelangelo penned a sardonic poem, expressing the extreme physical anguish he was undergoing while working on the celestial ceiling.

"My belly, tugged under my chin all out of whack. Beard points like a finger at heaven. Near the back of my neck, skull scrapes where a hunchback's lump would be."

The poem bears out the immense physical sacrifice he made for art. When Michelangelo undertook the monumental Sistine ceiling project, he was already famous for his marble masterpieces, *Pieta* and *David*. His letters to his father reveal the toils and troubles he had suffered "drudging about Italy" for over a decade, in order to further his family's fortunes "with the utmost

Portrait of Michelangelo at the Time of the Sistine Chapel, by Marcello Venusti, 1504-1506, Uffizi Galleries

injury and discomfort to myself." I have "borne every shame, suffered every hardship, worn my body out in every toil, put my life to a thousand hazards."

In the *sonetto caudato*, written between 1509-1510, he voices his torment with vivid, merciless black humor, finding himself "pigeon-breasted," "bent like a bow" and "Face dribbled…like a Byzantine floor mosaic."

Michelangelo was known for his cheeky sense of humor. Once asked why an artist had rendered an ox in a picture so lifelike, he replied, "Every painter can portray himself well." He delighted in reading poets such as Dante and Petrarch, and, throughout his long life, wrote reams of lyrical prose and amorous ditties to his mostly male friends.

After years of backbreaking work, it was as though he was getting even in words; setting the record straight for posterity:

"From all this straining my guts and my hambones tangle…Thank God I can swivel my butt about for ballast. Feet are out of sight; they just scuffle around, erratic. Up front my hide's tight elastic; in the rear it's slack and droopy, except where crimps have callused."

In the margin of his Sistine chapel agony poem, he sketched a caricature of himself, straining painfully to paint a little sprite on the diabolically out-of-reach ceiling, his head bent backwards as far as it could go.

With Michelangelo commandeered to Rome to work on the tomb of Pope Julius II, the Vatican architect Donato Bramante contrived for him to work instead on the Sistine. In *The Lives of the Artists*, Michelangelo's contemporary, the painter and art historian Giorgio Vasari, suggests Bramante aimed to humiliate the Florentine, who had no experience in

Michelangelo, sketch illustrating a sonnet decribing the painting of the Sistine Chapel, December 1508

frescos. He wanted to trip the bearded genius up, in favor of his friend, Raphael.

Rivalry and tensions ran more than Sistine-ceiling high among Rome's creative elite, yet Michelangelo apparently never let personal enmity enter the public sphere.

That is not to say he took it all lying down. Angry and upset at Bramante's interfering, he tried his hardest to get out of what he knew would be a grueling task, fleeing Rome briefly and nominating Raphael for the job instead. The ambitious pope, with his fearsome reputation as *"papa terribile,"* would have none of it, and eventually got his way.

Julius had Bramante set up scaffolding and bolt it to the ceiling — the architect must have purred with pleasure at the idea of figuratively nailing his enemy to the roof. Infuriated, Michelangelo dismantled the structure and designed his own workstation, a wooden platform 60 feet high that became a prototype — even for rivals.

Over four years, he painted the 6,000-square-foot surface, aided only by a plasterer and color-mixer. Vasari marveled at the way Michelangelo held up through the ordeal. "The work was executed in great discomfort, as Michelangelo had to stand with his head thrown back and he so injured his eyesight that for several months he could only read and look at designs in that posture."

Though Michelangelo "despised the discomfort" and grumbled loudly, his "thin and muscular" body was a great advantage.

Towards the completion of the fresco, in a letter to his brother Buonarroto, Michelangelo reveals the lengths to which he was ready to go to, in order to achieve perfection: "I am suffering greater hardships than ever man endured,

Pope Julius II ordering Bramante, Michelangelo and Raphael to construct the Vatican and St. Peter's, by Émile Jean-Horace Vernet, 1827, Musée du Louvre

ill, and with overwhelming labor; still I put up with all in order to reach the desired end."

Restless, ingenious and instinctive, the artist, whose brushstrokes and marbled curves dominated the Italian Renaissance, worked with astonishing energy, agility and speed.

"I could see the bristles from his brushes caught in the paint, and the mucky thumbprints he'd left along the margin," said British art critic Waldemar Januszczak, after scrutinizing the Sistine ceiling from the top of a television scaffold.

The pope's impatience with getting the work done may have had more fallout on the results than Michelangelo's physical sacrifices. When the artist said he would finish it only when it met his artistic sense, the pope threatened to pull the scaffolding down.

The latter lines of Michelangelo's sonnet suggest his fresco was distorted by the physical acrobatics, so the end result did not always do justice to his preparatory sketches: "Not odd that what's on my mind, when expressed, comes out weird, jumbled. Don't berate; no gun with its barrel screwy can shoot straight."

His corporal contortions also created spectacular artistic effect. Michelangelo covered the ceiling with a dramatic *trompe l'oeil*—a jam-packed, agitated canvas of larger-than-life, luridly colored biblical figures, tumbling from the ceiling.

In November 1536, at the age of 60, he was again "dumped destitute" in Rome, as he wrote in one verse, when Pope Clement called on him to paint the altar wall of the Sistine Chapel with the *Last Judgment*.

The electric cobalt blue-backed composition centers on a colossal and scary Christ, condemning many of his subjects to hell, while redeeming others. Swarming around him are several familiar religious figures: the Virgin, trumpeting angels, the Archangel Michael reading from the book of souls, St. Peter with his keys, St. Lawrence with the gridiron, and St. Bartholomew hanging onto his own hide—the latter is generally taken to be a self-portrait of the artist, who clearly considered himself a damned soul. This time around, Michelangelo's artistic license was put in check by the papal censures.

Judging the fresco more fit for bathrooms and inns than the papal chapel, the master of ceremonies under Pope Paul III, Biagio da Cesena, pressured for the shameful parts to be covered up. After Michelangelo's death in 1564, Daniele da Volterra got the job of painting over the private parts, earning him the nickname *Il braghettone*, "the breeches-maker." Michelangelo possibly avenged Biagio preemptively, painting him into the fresco as Minos—who has been consigned to Inferno with his snake-like tail biting at his genitals.

During the five years painting the *Last Judgment*, Michelangelo resorted to further poetic outpourings to describe the dire physical consequences of the work: his eyes filled with "mauve pigment pestled till its ground," and

The Last Judgement (detail), by Michelangelo, 1537-1541, Sistine Chapel

his body "packaged…like the pulp in fruit compacted by its peel. In lonely gloom, a genie in a jar."

He apparently worked so hard, and was so exhausted, that he sometimes failed to wash or undress for a week. Rheumatism, gout, arthritis, impaired vision, deafness, headaches, vertigo and cramps are on the incredible list of ailments he accumulated along the way, yet his long-suffering life was also one of remarkable stamina.

Michelangelo died in Rome in 1564, at the age of 89. His healthy, muscular body and good complexion in the last years of his life, wrote Italian biographer, Ascanio Condivi, in 1520, owed to his "natural constitution," exercise habits, and "habitual continence in food and sexual indulgence."

No doubt, he eased out his aching muscles and kept himself fit at the Roman baths. It was here he observed the physical perfection of virile, strapping bodies, whose influence can be seen rising into Heaven and descending into Hell in the *Last Judgment*.

CHAPTER 18.

TREASURES IN THE TIBER: THE LAVISH WORLD OF VILLA FARNESINA

1511

In the flamboyant, fertile era of the Italian Renaissance, noble banker and businessman Agostino Chigi built an art collection rivalling those of popes and cardinals. As financier and friend of Pope Julius II, between 1503 and 1513, Chigi "*il magnifico*" backed the pontiff's megalomaniac building boom, focusing on the beautification of the supremely powerful Papal State, the Patrimonium Petri (literally, the Patrimony of Peter).

The Sienna-born banker was renowned for his dazzling dinner parties, at which money was as trifling a concern as his exorbitant expenditures on art. The setting for these sumptuous, spectacle-filled summer nights was his Trastevere pleasure palace, the Villa Chigi—now Farnesina—which he had frescoed from floor to ceiling with works by Raphael and others.

Agostino envisaged the residence as a semi-rural *villa suburbana*, set within vast gardens of bergamot, cedars and cypresses on the Tiber's west bank. For the design, Chigi turned to Baldassarre Peruzzi, who had worked with Raphael on St. Peter's. The result was a harmonious arched façade concealed splendid columned halls with coffered ceilings, decorated with grotesques and mythical objects.

< *The Triumph of Galatea*, by Raphael, 1512, Villa Farnesina   119

Left: La Loggia; Right top: *Wedding Banquet of Cupid and Psyche*, by Raphael, 1517–18

The ground floor loggias of the Villa Farnesina were crowned with voluptuous frescos of flowers, fruits and cherubs, of love gods riding on dove-pulled chariots, and triumphant nymphs sailing through the sky on dolphin-towed conch shells. Raphael Sanzio and his team worked on these vaulted murals, in the Loggia di Psiche and Loggia di Galatea, for several years after the villa's completion in 1511.

The powerful and well-connected Chigi used his banking flair to develop a merchant business that extended from Rome to Constantinople and employed 20,000. As his attentions turned to lending money to popes, Chigi played a decisive financial role during the papacy of Giuliano della Rovere, better known as Julius II. Convinced the beautification of buildings would be a "formidable instrument" to assert Rome's supremacy as *caput mundi*, Julius II had launched of a frenzied building agenda that would last from 1503 to 1513. To achieve his dream, he ambitiously enlisted the Renaissance's leading lights: Michelangelo, Raphael and Pinturicchio.

Chigi, who enjoyed a very close relationship with "Giulio", started to contend with him, commissioning a small group of trusted painters and architects, most notably, Raphael, to work on his villa and public projects.

Marriage of Alexander and Roxane, by Il Sodoma, c. 1517, Villa Farnesina

The prestige of relatively unknown painters such as Sebastiano del Piombo—Michelangelo's mate and Raphael's rival, who Chigi enticed to Rome from Venice—snowballed with his patronage.

Chigi was the only secular patron vying with powerful cardinals and the papal court in the artistic bounty of the High Renaissance court—not only during the office of Julius II, but that of his successor, Leo X, the art-loving Giovanni de' Medici. His Villa Chigi became a preening ground of high society, especially for cultural movers and shakers, and Chigi had it decorated accordingly.

Raphael painted the immense vaulted ceiling of the central ground floor loggia with the *Cupid and Psyche*—a wedding banquet for Eros and the winged Psyche, festooned in flowers, leaves and fruits. It was in this splendid setting, opening onto the river and gardens, that Chigi held his own lavish banquets, entertaining popes, diplomats, artists and high-class courtesans.

Rivaling the feasts of imperial Rome, Chigi's parties were lauded for the copiousness and exoticism of food, and absolute fortune of precious

Romans During the Decadence, by Thomas Couture, 1847, Musée d'Orsay

tableware. Under a canopy of sensual works of art, guests were treated to first-rate theatrical and musical performances, and had the run of the palace and gardens—the Loggia di Galatea opened straight onto the *viridarium*, a pleasure garden of rare plants, bordering the riverside Lungotevere della Farnesina.

At the end of one evening-long bacchanalia, the banquet setting was demolished. In his determination to *fa la bella figura*, or make a good impression, Chigi wanted to ensure his guests' impressions were not tainted by the ennui of cleaning up.

To hell with the plate cleaning, and the tableware treasures; they can all go straight out the window into the Tiber, he said—that will take care of that. Gold plates, porcelain, silverware are easy to come by. The guests did as told and tossed their plates, leftovers, napkins and goblets out of the open windows and straight into the Tiber. A cunning Chigi had netted the riverbank, and sent divers out to recover anything that slipped through the net.

This kind of excessive behavior was not rare among rich families of Rome, and the frescos played a part by elevating the villa's owners to the rooftop in grandiose representations. Villa Chigi was smothered in homages to pagan and classical worlds, but also to the self. In 1511, Baldassarre Peruzzi painted the vault of the Loggia of Galatea with astrological figures representing Chigi's horoscope.

The View of the Villa Farnesina (right) and the Farnese garden, by Giuseppe Vasi, 1754

Upstairs in his bedroom, the fresco of the *Marriage of Alexander the Great and Roxana* by Raphael's follower "Sodoma" (the Sienese painter Givoanni Antonio Bazzi,) shows Chigi and his wife being undressed by lecherous cherubs.

Such grandstanding did not pay off; Chigi's profligate behavior eventually sent him bankrupt. That was the pitfall of living during the "golden age" of the Renaissance — such a fertile and carefree era, people did not see the storm clouds gathering.

THE FARNESE AND FARNESINA

Today the Villa Farnesina is in the hands of the Accademia Nazionale dei Lincei, attached to the cultural ministry. At the end of the 16th century, it was purchased by Cardinal Alessandro Farnese, and named Villa Farnesina, to distinguish it from the Farnese Palace located on the other side of the river.

The names of the Farnese and Farnesina, are still painfully close, and often confused. What distinguishes them the most, apart from the art—the works by Michelangelo at the latter, and those of his rival, Raphael, at Chigi's former residence—are the appetizing tales of a mercurial art patron and his riotous dinner parties.

CHAPTER 19

RAFFAELLO & THE BAKER'S DAUGHTER: THE PAINTER, THE MISTRESS, THE SECRET MARRIAGE

1518 - 1519

In the gloriously frescoed Palazzo Barberini, a spellbinding portrait by the High Renaissance artist Raffaello Sanzio hangs as a reminder of his mysterious love life.

La Fornarina, the beautiful dark-eyed baker's daughter, with crow-black hair, crescent eyebrows and cherubic lips, holds a transparent chiffon to her exposed chest, as she gazes teasingly, as though daring the onlooker to get her to drop her cover. The splendid black and gold silk turban, knotted on her head like a braided bread wreath, offsets her dark and beige tones.

The subject is presumably Margherita Luti, the daughter of a Siennese baker—*fornaio*—who frequently sat for Raphael at her home in Trastevere, on the other side of the Tiber. Painted around 1518, question marks have endured for centuries over Raffaello's precise relationship with his model, but there was definitely an intimate connection.

La Fornarina's revealing pose and beguiling gaze have led many to believe there was much more to the painter-muse relationship off-canvas—the band on her left arm, engraved with the artist's name, gives their game away.

Self Portrait, by Raphael, 1506, Uffizi Galleries

Raphael may have sought to cover up their liaison by painting over a wedding ring worn by *La Fornarina*. A ring on her left hand emerged during recent restoration— curators believe Raphael hid it deliberately, after reconsidering the marriage.

Possibly fate intervened to force him to do so. Though he officially died a bachelor, some art critics believe Raphael followed his heart, and secretly wedded his mistress, yet the marriage was hushed up by vested interests, who wished for his betrothal to Maria Bibbiena, the niece of a powerful cardinal.

Alternatively, the ring may have been erased to protect his reputation. Raphael was a consummate courtier, with deep aristocratic affiliations, and admitting to a romantic association with someone of such lowly class, would not have done his flourishing career any good.

When Raphael arrived in Rome in autumn 1508, at the height of the Renaissance, his talent was already well established. He came at the behest of Pope Julius II, probably after some whispering in his ear from the architect Donato Bramante, the painter's distant relative. Within no time he was accomplishing majestic frescos for popes and patricians, including Julius's private apartments

In 1514, Julius's successor, the art-loving Medici pope, Leo X, appointed Raphael chief architect of St. Peter's, and in the following year—on Bramante's death and wish—named him inspector of antiquities, invested with a tremendous purchasing power and responsibility. It was in this role that Raphael came face to face with the ancient Roman frescos (*grotteschi*), in the newly discovered cellars of Nero's Domus Aurea, which inspired his work immensely.

About the same time, he came to a gentleman's agreement with Cardinal Bibbiena—a close friend of both the painter and the pope—who had been

The School of Athens, by Raphael, 1510-11, Vatican Museums

pressuring the artist to marry for some time. For a generous dowry, Raphael accepted reluctantly to an open-ended engagement with the cardinal's niece, while continuing his dalliance with Luti.

Raphael's letters and sonnets, as well as the writings of his closest friend Baldassare Castiglione and the records of the 16th-century art historian Giorgio Vasari hint at this scenario.

The ill-fated love affair with Luti did wonders for Raphael's art, but he had no choice than to conceal it, for fear of offending his powerful patrons. In that case, Raphael may have disguised the ring, to guard the secret vow. Others guess that members of his atelier covered it up, to protect him posthumously—or on request from higher authorities. Clearly, the liaison was kept well under wraps at the time, even if some details have since emerged.

In his *Lives of the Artists*, Vasari writes that Raphael longed after a mystery woman to such an extent that he neglected his work. Raphael's off-canvas preoccupations, not only with *La Fornarina*, but the general pursuit of his "carnal delights", wrote Vasari, led him to rely strongly on members of his workshop to finish the frescos at the Villa Farnesina.

Vasari paints Raphael as a great sexual marauder and lady's man who—far from satisfied with his baker's delight—"kept up his secret love affairs and pursued his pleasures with no sense of moderation."

A child in Raphael's time, Vasari is known to exaggerate, yet he obviously feels that some of the artist's fleshy paintings of divine earthly beauties—which "seem more to be made of living flesh than of painted colours"—were life-inspired.

Left: *Raphael and La Fornarina*, by Jean Auguste Dominique Ingres, 1814, Fogg Art Museum, Cambridge; right: *The Betrothal of Raphael and the Niece of Cardinal Bibbiena*, by Jean Auguste Dominique Ingres, 1813-14, The Baltimore Museum of Art

Dilatory maybe, yet the love-struck painter was busy decorating some of Rome's most famous rooftops, ducking to-and-fro between Trastevere and the Vatican's papal apartments for several years between 1513 and 1518.

Work on the four Stanze di Raffaello, today within the Vatican Museum, was started in 1508 and finished by his team in 1524. The walls and ceilings of the rooms are painted with a suite of frescos depicting scenes from the Bible through medieval history, of learned Renaissance men and human virtues.

When Raphael was at work at the Villa Farnesina, Michelangelo, who was busy painting the Sistine ceiling, dropped by to keep abreast of the competition.

Given the villa's Trastevere location, Raphael could easily have whipped away for a little lunchtime intrigue to Luti's house.

The Trastevere restaurant Romolo nel Giardino della Fornarina is named in memory of the baker's daughter and her entanglement with Raphael, and it was here she posed for him. Being the artist's favorite model was a perfect alibi for their romantic rendezvous.

According to Vasari, the velvet-bereted maestro ended up arranging for Luti to move in with him at his Villa Farnesina quarters, in order to finish the work. He may even have snuck her into his Vatican digs.

Any risk of a change in conditions of his secret handshake with the cardinal, which might have prohibited him from continuing his affair, ended with Bibbiena's premature death, some say from a broken heart.

The tomb of Raphael and Maria Bibbiena in the Pantheon. The Madonna above the tomb is by Lorenzetto.

Her father's all-powerful pact seems to have outlived both his daughter and the artist. Raphael died soon after, aged 37, "having indulged in more than his usual excesses", wrote Vasari, and gripped by a tempestuous fever. A good Christian, he sent his mistress away from his deathbed, "giving her the means to live honestly."

Luti was forbidden to attend the funeral, while Raphael's overlooked bride-to-be lay by his side at the cemetery.

What became of the baker's daughter? Whispers of her joining a convent for fallen women, even killing Raphael, have run wild. Try as gossips might to discredit Margherita Luti, they have only added to her aura.

The painting *La Fornarina* has created a myth at the Palazzo Barberini. Raphael may have been the biggest peddler of the myth, agreeing to lie — and to paint lies — to conceal the fact that he and his beloved Margherita were married. Perhaps the money he earned by doing so guaranteed her a comfortable future.

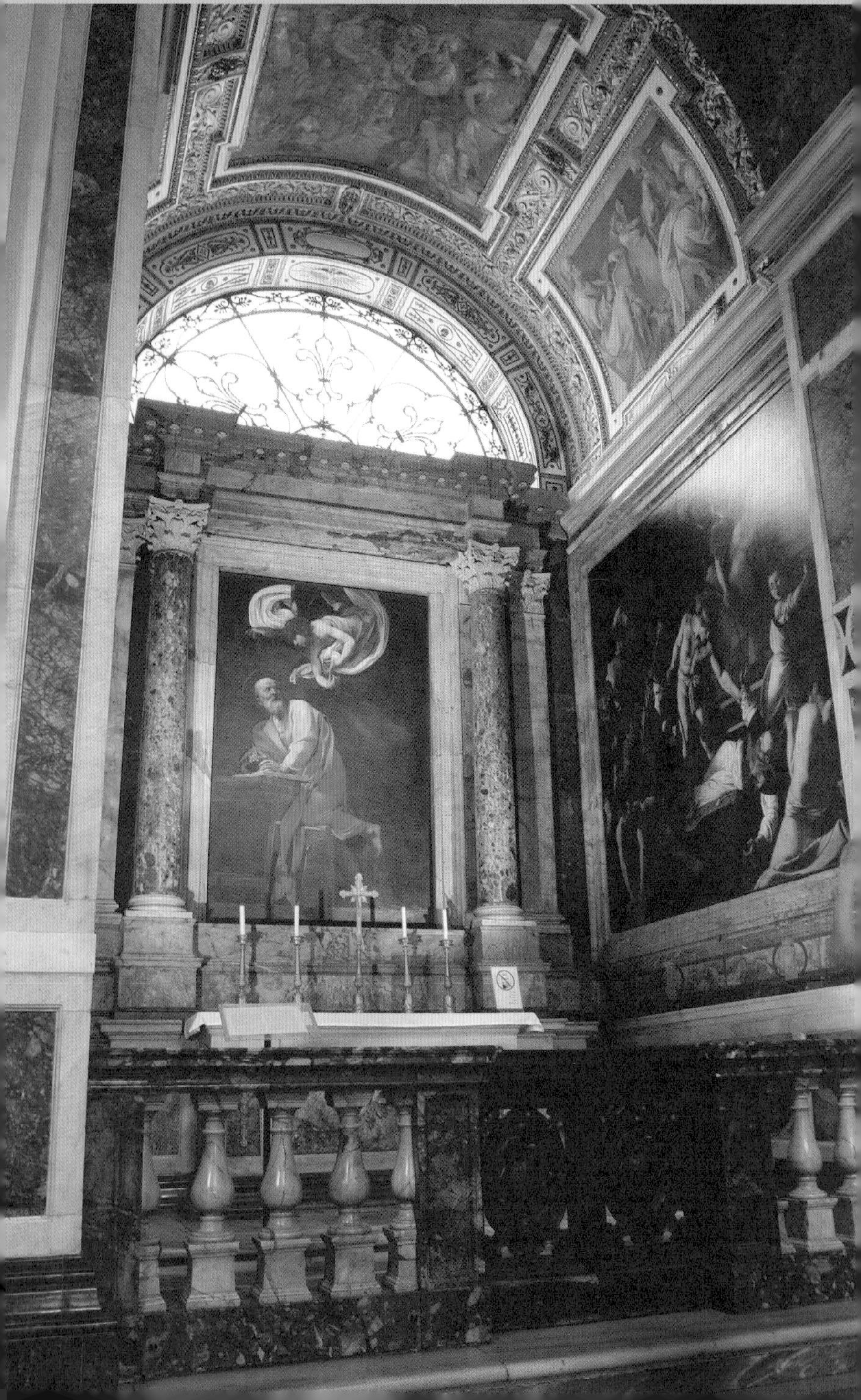

CHAPTER 20.

BRUTAL REALITY: CARAVAGGIO IN THE CAMPO MARZIO

1606

Michelangelo Merisi da Caravaggio's turbulent days in Rome were spent walking and painting on the dark side, in the shadowy streets of the Campo Marzio—the old medieval heart of Rome, extending between the Piazza di Spagna, the Piazza del Popolo, the Piazza Navona and the Tiber River. It was here the painter struggled to make his mark, rose to fame, and then fell into a self-destructive spiral.

The place Caravaggio chose as his stomping ground and combat zone had been used by ancient Romans to prepare for battle, and named after the God of War: the Campus Martius (Field of Mars), a vast floodplain, spreading from the Tiber River towards the Pincio and Quirinal hills.

During the Middle Ages, the area became the urban center of Rome, its dense hive of streets beautified in the 15th and 16th centuries with Renaissance squares, *palazzi*, fountains, basilica and churches.

When Caravaggio arrived from Milan in search of work, in late 1592, he landed in a cutthroat survivor's world, with an increasing number of artists vying for patronage of cardinals and secular sponsors.

Portrait of Michelangelo Merisi da Caravaggio, by Ottavio Leoni, c. 1621, Biblioteca Marucelliana, Florence

Popular and crowded downtown Rome was the easiest place for artists to make ends meet. By the 16th century, a community of some 100 painters had gathered here, renting rooms and *botteghe*—workshops—from the handful of cardinals who occupied its villas and palaces.

After a couple of destitute years, Caravaggio was taken under the wing of Cardinal Francesco Maria del Monte, a colorful and influential character who provided for him, in return for paintings to deck the walls of his palace in the Piazza Madama. Caravaggio's contact with the Cardinal was a blessing, guaranteeing him a string of commissions over several years, along with stipends and cushy lodgings in an upstairs room at the Palazzo Madama. (Built by the Medici family in the 16th century, the Palazzo Madama is now home to the Italian Senate.)

Nudging Piazza Navona, with the riverside Lungotevere Marzio on one side and the Pantheon on the other, his quarters lay in the thick of the Campo Marzio's commerce, marketplaces, shops and taverns. This zone framed his restless, riotous Rome years, his brilliant brushstrokes and his bawdy nighttime pranks.

Drawn into the cardinal's distinguished circle and lavish lifestyle, Caravaggio was also brushing with the shadowy side of life, befriending courtesans and using commoners or his skylarking companions as models. The sinewy Via della Scrofa, around which he spent his most tormented and violent period formed a backbone to his daily life in the city: its barbers, saddlers and painters' studios.

In 1600, at 27 years of age, he won his first public success, with a trio of paintings of St. Matthew on the walls of the Contarelli Chapel, in the church of San Luigi dei Francesi, a stone's throw from his home, down the narrow vicolo del Salvatore.

With the aid of a mirror, Caravaggio painted himself into the *Martyrdom of St. Matthew*, which depicts the slaying of Matthew by henchmen of the Ethiopian King Hirtacus, after he refused to pressure the virgin Princess Iphigenia into marrying the king—her uncle. Caravaggio's bearded face is wrought with sadness at the violence; the painter as a witness to abominable truths—it summed up his life.

Crucifixion of Saint Peter, 1601, by Caravaggio, Cerasi Chapel, Santa Maria del Popolo

Caravaggio's art like his life was marked by shocking realism—a warts-and-all, pitiless perception, which inflamed his genius and tragic demise.

Launching into two canvases for the Cerasi Chapel of the Church of Santa Maria del Popolo in Piazza del Popolo, he was heralded in cultural circles as the "*egregius in Urbe Pictor*," the outstanding painter of the city.

Dramatically lit in the artist's shadowy style, the dabbing of the *Crucifixion of St. Peter* and other martyr masterpieces were matched, brushstroke by brushstroke, by the dramatic intensity of his own life.

By night, he and his sword-carrying friends, a motley group of hot-blooded young painters, booksellers and papal couriers, headed out from Cardinal del Monte's residence and roamed around looking for trouble. Whoring, brawling and boozing, the would-be *cavaliere* (knights) pranced about from bar to brothel with bravado, under the motto *nec spe, nec metu*—no hope, no fear.

The same impetuous, passionate temperament that fired Caravaggio's creativity, got him into a quarrelsome cycle, intensifying from 1602, as he notched up a colorful police record of verbal and physical aggressions, fistfights and sword attacks, and ended up several times behind bars.

The outlaw artist was accused of throwing a plate of artichokes in a waiter's face at an inn on the Via Maddalena, and threatening him with a sword because he didn't like the dressing; he was imprisoned for throwing stones and insults at policemen near Via del Babuino; and arrested for possession of a sword and a dagger on the Via del Corso.

Police blotter sketch of Caravaggio's sword and dagger, carried without a permit, on his arrest, Saturday, May 28 1605

Dressed in noble yet tattered garments, and maintaining his entitlement to carry a sword, his success went to his already troubled head.

As his behavior became more erratic, so did his lodgings. In 1601, he moved to the palazzo of the Cardinal Girolamo Mattei, home to a fabulously wealthy banking family, on the Piazza Mattei, where he continued to unleash his sizzling creativity, while treading a blazing trail of destruction.

Paradoxically, as he became inextricably embroiled in a feuding world, Caravaggio was consecrating himself almost entirely to religious paintings, though the images were as full of the awfulness of human existence, *terribilita*, as his life.

Some of his works were rejected—their brutal naturalism shocked, and the paintings were judged offensive, yet both sacred and profane, by contemporary critics. The master of *chiaroscuro*—of light and dark—whose dramatic use of contrast influenced the likes of Rembrandt and Rubens, was ahead of his times.

In March 1605, he rented a house in the Vicolo dei Santi Cecilia e Biagio (now the Vicolo del Divino Amore) forever nudging closer, in time and distance, to his fateful Roman finale.

Over the next few months, he painted up a dramatic street theater: drawing a sword on a lawyer who rivaled for the attentions of his courtesan girlfriend and favorite model, Lena; pelting stones at his landlady's windows after she sued him for making holes in his ceiling to store his paintings; and

The Death of the Virgin, by Caravaggio, 1601-1603, Musée du Louvre

recovering from knife wounds at the home of his friend, Andrea Ruffetti, claiming he fell on his sword.

The next year, he committed the crime from which there would be no return, fatally stabbing the pimp Ranuccio Tomassoni, in a fight in via della Pallacorda. The motives for the skirmish are hazy — possibly a dual sparked by rivalry over a prostitute who Caravaggio used as model, perhaps an honor killing, self-defense, the reaction to a terrible insult, or a terrible accident.

Shortly after, in May 1606, the self-destructive genius, who lived life as combat, fled Rome seriously wounded, with a death sentence — *banda capital* — upon his head. After four tormented years on the run, he died, presumably from heat exhaustion and infected wounds, on a wild Tuscan beach.

Caravaggio was 38 — he was on his way back to Rome, in a boat laden with art works for a new patron, having finally secured a papal pardon for the killing.

On and off canvas, violence and darkness awaited him at every turn, in place of light and redemption.

The Campo Marzio will never shake Caravaggio's image, and the shadow of a virtuoso street thug will lurk forever in its *vicolo* and *via*, as much as in the churches and chapels, galleries and palazzo where his works hang.

CHAPTER 21.

ARTEMISIA GENTILESCHI: CREATIVE DESIRES ON THE VIA DELLA CROCE

1611

In the male-dominated art world of the Italian Baroque, Artemisia Gentileschi rose to be the most famous female painter, and painter of women. Born in 1593, she spent her youth in the Campo di Marzio at the height of the Caravaggesque years, when many artists, including her father, Orazio, came under Caravaggio's influence. Courageously refusing to live in the shadow of male colleagues—and as a victim of their violence—she excelled by exerting her talents over patrons and lovers. Her paintings of heroic women avenging brutally on men also helped settle the scores for the sexes.

Artemisia Gentileschi was born into art. The daughter of Orazio Gentileschi, an artist-pal of Caravaggio, she was raised in the artists' quarter of Rome, surrounded by art academies, studios and churches, where her father painted frescoes.

During her youth, her family moved several times through this honeycomb of medieval streets, from Via di Ripetta to the Piazza di Spagna and Via Margutta. In the years following her mother's death during childbirth on Boxing Day 1605, the Gentileschis moved to Via della Croce.

< *Self-portrait as the Allegory of Painting*, by Artemisia Gentileschi, 1638-9, Royal Collection, UK

Portrait of Orazio Gentileschi, by George Vertue, 1684-1756,

Caravaggio and Gentileschi senior were part of the "clique of Via della Croce," sued in 1603 by the painter Giovanni Baglione for defamatory poems circulating among Rome's artists, which satirized him as "Gian Coglione" (John the prick) and described his work as excrement.

Caravaggio visited Orazio's studio often to borrow brushes and other painting material, and his violent realism left as indelible an impression on young Artemisia as the idealism of the Tuscan school from which her father sprung.

Cruel reality surged through her veins, fed by the milieu in which she grew up as much as the tumultuous events of her own early life, starting with maternal loss.

Denied access as a woman to professional academies, by her late teens her talent—evidenced in works such as *Susanna and The Elders*, which she painted at 17—had turned many heads.

After she apprenticed with her father from 1605 to 1610, he lobbied hard to market her art, claiming in a letter to Cristina di Lorena, the Grand Duchess of Tuscany, that his 19-year-old daughter had already achieved works, which possibly outstrip some of "the leading *maestro* of this profession."

Her father was still unaware of the dark events of the previous year that would mark Artemisia for the rest of her life. In May of 1611, she was raped in the family's house by the landscape painter Agostino Tassi—her tutor, and a close friend and colleague of her father.

Legal action started with her father's appeal to the pope, stating that his daughter had been "forcibly deflowered and carnally known over and over." He accused his fellow Florentine of "rape and pimping."

After the first rape, Tassi played on her naivety and tricked her into thinking they were married—*more uxorio* (in the manner of man and wife)—and continued to take advantage of her.

"This is the ring and these the promises you gave me," she cried out at him during a five-month trial, laying bare his unscrupulous manipulation. In the process of standing up to him she was denounced for defamation of Tassi's character, publicly besmirched and tortured with sibille strings or thumbscrews, tightened around her fingers, in order to establish the truth.

Susanna and the Elders, by Artemisia Gentileschi, 1610, Schloss Weissenstein, Pommersfelden

Tassi refused to marry Artemisia, on the grounds that he was already married—in court it emerged he had hired assassins in an attempt to kill his wife after she ran off with her lover. Despite a criminal record of rape, sodomy, theft, debt and incest charges (the latter for impregnating his sister-in-law), Tassi got off lightly, returning to a thriving workshop after several months in prison, with plenty of commissions from prestigious Roman families.

Artemisia, on the other hand, had to redeem herself in the public eye. Within weeks she married Florentine artist Pierantonio Stiattesi and moved to his hometown. Here she was to enjoy considerable success over the coming decade, masterfully maneuvering her way to become the first woman accepted into the Accademia di Belle Arti, founded by Cosimo I de' Medici in 1563. There she rubbed shoulders with the artocracy, writing letters and waxing lyrical to influential artists and patrons.

In her early days in Florence, she completed one of her most famous paintings, *Judith Beheading Holofernes*—a Caravaggio retake, depicting the brutal slaughter of an Assyrian general by Jewish woman and her maid

Judith Beheading Holofernes, by Artemisia Gentileschi, 1611-12, Museo di Capodimonte, Naples

against a snow-white sheet. The fact this graphically violent canvas began during the Tassi trial, suggests that it took Artemisia no time to find a dazzling and cathartic way of avenging men through her work.

Refusing to play the victim, Rome's great *pittoressa* of women, revisited the same theme throughout her life, portraying biblical and mythical women as heroes, warriors and pitiless executioners.

Her violent depictions of Sisera nailing the head of Yael, Delilah rendering Samson powerless by cutting off his locks, Lucretia committing suicide after being raped by a sovereign's son, and King David's adultery with Bathsheba, are those of an artist acting out her most gruesome fantasies of retaliation against men, with a paintbrush as her primary weapon. In her lushly colored paintings, she trounces the would-be oppressor—yet it was the idea of giving in to men that was the real object of her wrath, rather than men themselves.

Indeed, it would seem she empowered herself by manipulating men with her charm. In 2011, thirty-five of her previously unpublished letters were discovered in an historic archive in Italy. As well as those wooing patrons— Cosimo II, Ferdinand II de' Medici, the Sicilian collector Antonio Ruffo and Duke Francesco I d'Este—there were letters to her lover, Francesco Maria Maringhi.

Written between 1617 and 1620, her intimate, candid correspondence with

Yael and Sisera, by Artemisia Gentileschi, 1620, Budapest Museum of Fine Art

the Florentine businessman reveals a passionate relationship, marked by jealousy and a deep distrust of men.

"I am well aware of all you are up to, and I know when you go to a woman, and when you go to the *osteria* (tavern)", Gentileschi charges at Maringhi, "You, my enemy, who so fraudulently makes out as a lover!"

While seriously questioning Maringhi's loyalty, she used him as an agent to solicit sponsors and do the legwork for connections with aristocratic patrons. Soon enough, Gentileschi separated from Stiattesi, (who had not only turned a blind eye, but encouraged the affair), and returned to Rome.

Over the next three decades leading up to her death in Naples in 1652, she lived an itinerant life: through several changes of address in Rome, a move to Naples where she ran a workshop, and time on and off with Maringhi in both.

Between 1638 and 1639 she lived in London attending to her ailing father who was a painter in the court of Charles I, and most likely spent other periods in Florence, Genoa and Venice.

It was as though Artemisia was not going to accept to be a captive to any place or anyone. Instead she spent her whole life liberating herself in movement and art.

CHAPTER 22

CARDINAL ART: SCIPIONE BORGHESE AT THE VILLA BORGHESE

1613

In 1617, Cardinal Scipione Borghese dropped by the Rome studio of the artist Domenico Zampieri. "Domenichino" was working on *La Caccia di Diana* (Diana's Hunt), a dreamy landscape showing the goddess Diana bathing with her naked nymphs, as her entourage partakes in a leisurely archery contest and prance through fields in golden draperies.

The painting is a pastiche of Roman legends: the warriors from Virgil's epic 1st-century B.C. poem, *Aeneid*, replaced by Diana, the Roman goddess of chastity.

It so tickled Scipione, he offered to buy it on the spot, but the work was already spoken for. Diana had been commissioned by Cardinal Pietro Aldobrandini, his powerful predecessor, who was still rivaling him from the edge of the ring.

Domenichino refused to cave in to the insistent cardinal, so Scipione threw him in jail for a few days—long enough for Borghese to run off with the painting and tuck it away in his expanding collection of art and antiquities.

‹ *Apollo and Daphne*, by Gian Lorenzo Bernini, 1622-25, Galleria Borghese

The Hunt of Diana, by Domenichino, 1616-17, Galleria Borghese

Curiously, the bows and arrows in his latest acquisition were intended as a visual metaphor for shrewd, on-target debate.

Borghese may well have argued why he felt the painting was rightfully his, before he took it by force. It was not the only occasion that acquiring art to deck the hallways, gardens and walls of his villa meant stealing it. Banking on powerful papal connections, the covetous cardinal assembled one of Europe's finest art collections and a multi-million dollar fortune.

Born in 1576, into a wealthy family of bankers, Borghese's art-purchasing spree got off the starting block when his uncle Camillo Borghese became Pope Paul V in 1605.

With the ruthlessness that ran in the family, Camillo began his reign by having a writer who unflatteringly compared the former pope, Clement VIII, to the Emperor Tiberius beheaded on the Ponte Sant'Angelo.

Next, he ordained his nephew as a priest and fast-tracked his promotion to cardinal. Showering him with princely titles, lucrative offices and papal

Bust of *Cardinal Scipione Borghese*, by Gian Lorenzo Bernini, 1630, Galleria Borghese

handouts, Scipione Borghese "amassed one of the most astounding personal fortunes of the entire century," wrote Bernini biographer Franco Mormando.

Tugged along on the papal robes of his uncle, Borghese's average annual income for the three decades until his death in 1633 was over 200,000 *scudi*, the equivalent of 8 million dollars today.

The satin-cloaked clergyman used this immense purchasing power to become the most powerful art and property investor of his times, while helping artists, namely sculptor Gian Lorenzo Bernini, get off the ground. With almost unbridled support from Camillo, a passionate patron of the arts himself, Scipione acquired masterpieces to beautify the family palazzo on Quirinal Hill. The value of the private collection way surpassed that of the Vatican's art treasures, though much of it had been attained with most unholy means.

Ruthless and gluttonous in his appetite for art, Scipione went to extraordinary lengths to obtain his heart's desire. Domenichino was lucky— at least he was paid. That had not been the case several years earlier for the painter, Giuseppe Cesari, the Cavaliere d'Arpino. Cesari had caught the pope's attention with his exquisite designs for the mosaic ornamentation on the cupola of St. Peter's. No doubt, Borghese's beady eyes had settled hungrily on his collection.

In 1607, papal authorities stripped Cesari of a life's collection of paintings— some one hundred canvases, including early works by Caravaggio, who had trained in his studio. Cesari was thrown in jail on a hyped up charge of tax fraud, and his paintings seized. What Scipione wanted, he got.

During his decades of collecting, art often placed him beyond the law.

The Deposition (Pala Baglione, Borghese Deposition), by Raphael, 1507, Galleria Borghese

In 1608, with a nod from his uncle, he arranged for thieves to break into the Baglione family chapel in Perugia during the night, to obtain a panel from Raphael's painting *The Deposition* for his collection.

On another occasion, he procured over seventy canvases from competitor collector, Cardinal Sfondrati, but never coughed up the money.

In 1613, Scipione augmented the Borghese holdings with the purchase of a vineyard on the Pincio Hill, the ancient Collis Hortulorum—hill of the gardens. It was here he established the Villa Borghese as a magnificent summer residence in which to showcase his art and hold high-flying receptions. Today just a hop, skip and jump from the church of Trinità dei Monti and Spanish Steps, back then it was part of rural Rome, the campagna Romana.

Obsessed with taking out Cardinal Aldobrandini and his family, Borghese bribed the equivalent of two million dollars out of him in 1614.

The ill-gotten gains allowed the big-hearted *bon vivant* some heavy investments in sculptures and paintings for his new residence.

The villa was filled with pieces of ancient, Renaissance and Baroque art; the prelate had a particular passion for antique sculpture, and went mad allocating commissions to his favorite young talent, Bernini, between 1619 and 1624. Bernini undertook four life-size sculptures for Borghese, including the famous *Apollo and Daphne*. His depiction of the Greek nymph escaping the sun god's lustful grip by turning into a laurel tree shook up conservative church circles with its stony sensuality.

Galleria Borghese

On top of securing priceless assets for his collection, befriending Bernini was a great PR exercise for scandalous Scipione, one sorely needed after scandals over his personal life, and much publicized philandering with the Monsignor Stefano Pignatelli.

Borghese clearly had a marble fetish, and it was Bernini or bust. Two portrait sculptures of him by the Baroque star show his curls neatly trimmed about a four-cornered cardinal's cap, goatee, astute eyes and fleshy face.

If Borghese was seeking immortality, he got it. Realized the year before his death, the oversized portrait busts are so lifelike, it is as though he were there in the room.

Bernini almost split the first statue in two with a chisel by accident, not long before the cardinal was due to collect it. The marble *maestro* rapidly threw together another, which naturally Borghese preferred to the disfigured version.

The busts also perpetuate a paradox: Borghese looks magnanimous, every bit the sensualist he was purported to be—"a vital, congenial personality, stout from good eating, deeply devoted to art, and civilized pleasure," wrote historian Robert Torsten Petersson in *Bernini and the Excesses of Art*— whereas his art heists and embezzlements read like criminal record.

While history often sullies him, Bernini elevated Borghese in marble.

CHAPTER 23.

SCULPTING ROME: BERNINI, BORROMINI & THE BAROQUE EPOCH

1646

Piazza Navona puts the brilliance of the Baroque's two greatest rivals on show. Within arm's reach of Gian Lorenzo Bernini's *Fontana dei Quattro Fiumi* is Francesco Borromini's glorious façade and crowning cupola on the Chiesa di Sant'Agnese in Agone. Borromini spent most of his life feeling he had been overshadowed by the Baroque superstar. His torment ended when he threw himself on his sword at the age of 68, leaving Bernini to outshine him for another two decades.

Contained within the Vatican's secret archives are notices of payment to Gian Lorenzo Bernini, made between October 10, 1669 and February 1670, in the latter years of the virtuoso sculptor's life—decades after his meteoric rise to sculptor stardom in his early twenties, his dramatic and almost fatal fall from papal grace, and his miraculous creative resurrection.

Thus was the level of involvement between certain church leaders and the Baroque epoch's blistering talent; there was reason for it to be kept under lock and key for several centuries. Vatican connections could make or break an artist's fortunes in the 17th century, and could change in a wink with a switch of pope or if the church no longer felt it was banking on brilliance.

*Gian Lorenzo Bernini,
Self-Portrait*, c. 1623,
Galleria Borghese

Which is precisely what happened to Bernini: despite spectacular early success in the pope's inner circles, his career and personal life went dangerously off the rails in his late forties.

Bernini arrived in Rome in 1605, as a 7-year-old prodigy. Within a year, Paul V hailed him the next Michelangelo after observing the artist sketch with velocity the head of St. Paul. With one of his most famous sculptures, *David*, under his belt by the age of 21, and *Apollo and Daphne* four years later, the dashing artist captured the hearts of popes and other rich private patrons with his vigorous, soul-stirring, seemingly flesh-and-blood sculptures.

Knighted by Gregory XV in 1621, and henceforth called "*il Cavaliere*", Bernini was chummy with the greatest patrons of the era, Cardinal Scipione Borghese and Cardinal Maffeo Barberini—the latter supported Bernini through his two decades as Pope Urban VIII starting in 1623.

A charismatic, clever courtier, Bernini excelled at gliding through the political quicksand and scoring commissions, whereas his greatest rival, the brilliant but embittered architect Francesco Borromini, floundered.

In 1624, Urban VIII handed Bernini the plum job of redesigning the *baldacchino* canopy over the altar of St Peter's. Unveiled in 1633, his flamboyant bronze creation stands upon twisted candy columns, festooned with cherubs, laurel leaves and smiling suns.

Behind the scenes, there was rising bitterness about Bernini's monopolization of 17th-century artistic life, with many artists complaining of the difficulty of finding work without his blessing. No one was brooding more than Borromini, who lived most of his life in Bernini's shadow. Bernini was an amiable go-getter; Borromini, one year his junior, was reclusive and touchy.

Borromini had always played a subordinate role to Bernini, first working on the Palazzo Barberini, then under Bernini in the top job as architect of St.

Left: Anonymous portrait of a young Borromini; Right: *St Peter's*, by Viviano Codazzi, c. 1630, Prado Museum, showing Bernini's bell towers

Peter's, for which Borromini, as a trained architect, felt far better qualified. Bernini's cavalier treatment of Borromini, and his failure to give him credit for contribution to his designs, only rubbed salt into the wounds.

Bernini had no reason in turn to be jealous, and he knew it. Other than almighty talent he had the pope's benediction: "Bernini was made for Rome, and Rome for Bernini," Urban VIII declared in an official apostolic letter issued in the early 1640s.

The papal bull aimed to keep Bernini away from the temptation of being wooed permanently to the French court—he accepted the invitations much later, spending several months at court of King Louis XIV in 1655.

For Urban VIII, Bernini was a great asset, and he was not about to let him slip through his fingers, prophetically describing him as "a rare man…a sublime artificer, born by divine Disposition and for the glory of Rome to illuminate the century."

The instinctive, fiery nature which faceted his work, however, would almost be his undoing. Bernini's badness erupted when he had the face of his model and sculpting assistant's wife, Costanza Bonarelli, brutally disfigured. Bernini was gripped by a fit of vengeful rage, when he discovered his brother Luigi was also sharing Costanza's favors and sensual fervors. He

Ecstasy of Saint Teresa (detail), by Gian Lorenzo Bernini, 1647-52, Santa Maria della Vittoria

sent a thuggish envoy to do the dirty work, after spying on Costanza, and seeing Luigi depart from her residence early one morning.

To add insult to injury, Costanza not only had her beautiful face viciously slashed, she was imprisoned for adultery.

Bernini narrowly escaped a fate similar to that of Caravaggio, when a group of onlookers prevented him from killing Luigi, in a distraught frenzy, with an iron bar.

The pope came to Berinini's aid, ordering that he get married, as a form of punishment for his crimes. Things nevertheless went strangely downhill for Bernini from then, as though a higher than papal power was not letting him so easily off the hook.

The first cracks in his career came with those in St. Peter's façade; the assignment in 1637 to add bell-towers to the basilica shot Borromini's resentment sky-high. When a fissure appeared after the first tower was in place, Borromini feasted on Bernini's humiliation, accusing him of incompetence and providing evidence to authorities that the towers were doomed, as they had been built on shaky ground.

When the tower was demolished in 1646, so briefly, was Bernini's golden-boy image. His staunchest supporter, Pope Urban VIII, died and the new pope, Innocent X, ushered in his favorite: Francesco Borromini.

Innocent X started out giving preferential treatment to Borromini, but the architect would soon be licking his wounds again. Bernini's resurrection came in less than a year, with a sculpture commission from Cardinal

Bernini's Ponte Sant'Angelo *Angels* from 1669

Federico Cornaro, for his family chapel in the Santa Maria della Vittoria church.

The *Ecstasy of Saint Teresa* set Rome on fire: the nun with her head tilted back, and mouth ajar in rapture, gowns convulsing in ripples of stone, a smiling angel with an arrow standing overhead.

In the Middle Ages, Teresa graphically described having her entrails penetrated by an angel with a flame-tipped spear. Bernini's masterpiece brazenly confounds religious and sexual ecstasy.

Bernini was back with a vengeance. Innocent X subsequently picked his design over that of Borromini's for the centerpiece *Fontana dei Quattro Fiumi* in Piazza Navona. The only way to resist Bernini, quipped the pope, was not see his designs.

The aquatic theater Bernini designed—with its spouting cherubs, playful dolphins, and kneeling tritons trumpeting water through conch shells—was a prototype for many future fountains. From that point until his death in 1680, Bernini triumphed yet again; he was commissioned to complete St. Peter's Square in 1655, and in his seventies, the much-loved angels on the Ponte Sant'Angelo.

Walking around Rome, its major public squares and bridges, basilicas and chapels, Bernini accompanies you more than any artist. From St. Peter's colonnade to the fountains in the piazzas di Spagna, del Popolo and Barberini, he shaped Rome's look. A rivaling contribution comes from Borromini; history has ironically turned these adversaries into allies of a kind—co-creators of Rome's enduring Baroque beauty.

CHAPTER 24.

QUEEN CHRISTINA: A RUNAWAY ROYAL AT THE PALAZZO CORSINI

1654

In 1654, 28-year-old Swedish queen, Christina Vasa, abdicated and fled to Rome dressed as a man. Converting to Catholicism, she became a Vatican favorite and cardinal's sweetheart, living the high life at her papal-provided quarters. Flamboyant, feminist and controversial, Christina patronized the arts and science, while making her presence felt with her unorthodox views and behavior.

Born in 1626, Christina was the only child of King Gustavus Adolphus, known as the "Lion of the north" for his role as Protestant champion on Europe's church-split battlefields during the Thirty Years' War. Her mother, Maria Eleonora of Brandenburg, rejected her at birth, deeply upset that the child was not a boy. Her father displayed no such disappointment, but raised her as if she were.

Her father's decision to educate her as a boy played a determining hand in Christina's destiny. The skills she acquired during her youth—in warfare, languages and diplomacy—propelled her on a single-minded, unorthodox and rebellious path, while equipping her with the political and cultural savvy that would serve her for the rest of her life.

< *Portrait of Queen Christina Dressed In Roman Costume With Burgundy Sheath*, by David Klöcker von Ehrenstrahl (1629-1698).

Queen Christina of Sweden on Horseback, by Sébastien Bourdon, 1653

Having ensured the youth's education was on the right track, the "manly, sincere character," as he was described by a biographer in 1852, King Gustavus went off and died in battle, leaving his 5-year-old daughter to inherit the crown.

Providing her with an upbringing reserved for European men of her time was a sign of Gustavus's devotion, and the adoration was mutual. At a precocious age, Christina had to put aside the loss of her father, to assume royal duties. It was more of a double loss, living with the knowledge that her mother "could not stand the sight" of her, because she was "a girl and ugly," as Christina later claimed.

Happy to be a tomboy, she grew up surrounded by men, headstrong and bossy, and declared herself to be averse to "all that women do and say." At 14, she could speak six languages, rule a government and handle a gun, sword and horse. Entirely lacking in the one feminine attribute her father had hoped her to inherit, that of humility, she shamelessly bossed about her legislature.

Within eight years of her official crowning, in 1644 at age 18, after beckoning brilliant scholars including René Descartes to her court, and helping to end the religious warring between the Protestants and Catholics, she suffered a nervous breakdown.

During this period, she played an important hand in the 1648 Peace of Westphalia, a peace treaty that ended Europe's religious warring and promoted the Catholic cause. She also began harboring serious doubts about the Lutheran faith of her subjects, and neglecting official responsibilities

Celebrations for Christina of Sweden at Palazzo Barberini on February 28, 1656, by Filippo Gagliardi and Filippo Lauri, 1656

in favor of more libertine, colorful ways.

Definitely not the marrying kind, Christina vowed to leave the throne to her cousin Charles, rather than produce any heirs. (The 1933 film *Queen Christina* toyed tepidly with her contested sexuality, when Greta Garbo, as the sovereign, kisses her lady-in-waiting, Countess Ebba Sparre, on the lips.)

In a portrait of her on a rearing horse, by her court painter Sébastien Bourdon, she appears manly, with shoulder-length hair and riding coat. The cross-dressing queen, as she has been dubbed, groomed and spoke more like a man, wearing simple skirts and a man's jacket, topped off by a black velvet cap decorated with royal crests. Dressed in this manner, she left the country on horseback under the assumed name Count Dohna within a week of her abdication ceremony at Uppsala Castle, on May 30, 1654.

Disillusioned with Protestant intolerance, religious and personal convictions pulled her to Rome, where she was welcomed as a superwoman the following year, after converting to Catholicism mid-journey. The northern entry to Rome, the Porta del Popolo was specially beautified for her arrival on December 23, 1655, with Bernini commissioned to redecorate the gateway's façade, incorporating a Latin welcome inscription to the queen.

After riding into Rome from the Via Flaminia, flanked by two cardinals— Orsini and Costaguti—her ceremonial cavalcade continued to St. Peter's where she dismounted in the square, as the cannons of Castel Sant'Angelo fired.

Her reputation as an extraordinary diplomat, erudite in both the arts and sciences, gave her an immediate entrée into elite circles.

Though she had chosen to throw off the shackles of governing her own

Cardinal Decio Azzolino

country, Christina retained her royal title and was fiercely interested in Roman affairs and the intrigues of the Papal States.

How strange, that the woman born into the religious battles of the "Golden King", as Italians called her father, was now a darling of the Roman Catholic Church.

In 1659, her friend Pope Alexander VII set her up in style in a splendid residence in Trastevere, built for Renaissance Cardinal Raffaele Riario in 1511. Her street-facing lair has a double vaulted ceiling, divided by antique yellow faux marble columns. Each vault sports florid bible scenes: the story of Moses on one side, and Solomon on the other, framed within gilded cornices, and broken up by symbols of the Riario family heraldry. In another fresco of the three theological virtues, faith, hope and charity, the latter is represented by a virtuous cardinal.

There is a certain irony here, as the Queen had struck up an association with Cardinal Decio Azzolino, which left tongues wagging about a possible love affair, and forced the cardinal to reassure the pope that all was innocent. The two were close friends for life; Christina wrote Azzolino letters and arranged a papal exception from a rule preventing ladies from entertaining high-ranking church members in private.

The extraordinary location of the queen's lodgings, near the Tiber and over the hill from the Vatican, gave her an incredible vantage point for immersing in Rome's religious and cultural life.

A patron of the theater, music and science, she inspired the creation of the Arcadian Academy, whose members first met in the Riario villa's gardens the year after her death to discuss art and literature. In the three decades Queen Christina spent at the Riario palazzo until her death in 1689, she enriched the home with her own collection of paintings and sculptures.

Palazzo Corsini, by Giuseppe Vasi, 1754

Her cultural contributions outshone sporadic notoriety, caused by her over indulging in outlandish caprices: One tale attributes a dint in the doors of Villa Medici on Pincio Hill to Queen Christina firing a canon-ball in anger from the other side of the Tiber, because her cardinal was late for a meeting. Other racy reports have her falling in love with cardinals and nuns alike.

Though erratic and impetuous, she seems to have kept her eccentricity largely in check with dignified behavior. In 1656, her mad-as-a-hatter monarchical desires briefly outshone her Christian ones, and she plotted with the French to become the Queen of Naples. The church forgave her the brief disgrace she caused, and, upon her death, at age 62 in 1689, laid her to rest alongside popes and other sovereigns in the Vatican Grottoes below *St. Peter's.*

Though she turned her back on her dynasty, Queen Christina never forgot her Swedish identity, or her sentimental attachment to the country. In exile, she wrote love-letters to Sparre, "*la belle comtesse*", declaring her eternal devotion.

Liberated enough to be unconcerned by a lack of reciprocal love, she seems to have at least won the affection of her compatriots for following her true calling. Far from resenting their runaway royal, liberal Swedes hold her up proudly as their independent, feminist, Christian Queen, who held court in Catholic Rome.

CHAPTER 25.

THE GRAND TOUR AND CAFFÈ GRECO: GOETHE

1786—1788

At 3 a.m. on September 3, 1786, German writer Johann Wolfgang von Goethe slid through the "eternal gloomy fog" he so much wanted to escape and across the Bohemian border. His celebrated Italian journey began in a mail coach, under the assumed identity Jean Philippe Moller, a merchant from Leipzig. At 37, he was seeking more than a brief interlude; he was on a quest for personal and creative renewal—and he found it, living many months in Rome, "like a dream of youth."

Since the enormous literary success of *The Sorrows of Young Werther* (*Die Leiden des jungen Werthers*), a decade before, Goethe longed to take a break from the boredom of his administrative duties at the court of Weimar, and immerse himself in the creative inspiration of Roman antiquities and art.

Sneaking away from a holiday weekend at the spas of Carlsbad, having secured indefinite leave from his employer, he planned to join his artist, scholar and poet friends living in Rome during their Grand Tour of Europe.

After travelling via Trento, Verona, Vicenza, Venice, Bologna and Florence, Goethe passed through the Porta del Popolo on October 29, and straight into

Johann Wolfgang Von Goethe in Rome Looking out of the Window, by Wilhelm Tischbein, 1787

the cosmopolitan cultural scene. "I am in the land of the artists," he exclaimed finding himself in a milieu of some eighty painters.

One of their main haunts was L'Antico Caffè Greco in Via Condotti—Casanova was among the first guests to the famous literary café when it opened its doors in 1760.

In Goethe's day, it was referred to as the Caffe Tedesco (the German café) because it had become a colony for about two dozen of his compatriots—German intellectuals and painters, all of whom were said to be broke.

These bohemians wiled away hours imbibing espresso at the Caffè Greco, philosophizing about art and the creative process, and opining on the relative merit of Michelangelo and Raphael. In his memoirs in 1833, Goethe referred to the stimulant as "that liqueur which kept us awake several hours."

They gathered around the white marble-topped benches of the Omnibus—a long art-filled salon at the rear of the café, named because of its vague resemblance to a stagecoach.

Between coffees, Goethe walked, and absorbed the city by foot, in relative anonymity, having switched his *nom de plume* to that of painter Filippo Möller.

In a year, he visited over two hundred historic sites, from Renaissance piazza and palazzo to ancient tombs, theaters and temples, and was bowled over by what he saw. "I just keep my eyes open, look, and go, and come again," he wrote in his diaries, "for only in Rome can one prepare oneself for Rome."

Casa di Goethe at Via del Corso, 18

Goethe described the admiration he felt, not just attending mass at St. Peter's and climbing its dome, but in many encounters with Renaissance and ancient Rome, as a spiritual experience: "For reverence for a worthy object is always accompanied by a religious feeling."

His painter friend, Wilhelm Tischbein, sometimes accompanied him about Rome, as he drew statues and ruins—his main preoccupation during his stay, more than writing.

Towards the end of his first Roman *soggiorno*, in January 1787, he met the painter Angelica Kauffmann, an "inestimable woman", who became a life-long confidante.

Returning to Rome in June after travels in southern Italy, he often visited the home she shared with her painter husband painter, Antonio Zucchi. Angelica was a *succès fou* (a big hit) in Rome, and incredibly well connected, as she had been in her London years where in the 1770s she was one of two female

Artists in the Caffè Greco in Rome, by Ludwig Johann Passini, 1856, Hamburger Kunsthalle

founding members of the Royal Academy of Arts, alongside thirty-six men.

Kauffmann tired to paint Goethe, but "much to her chagrin", could not do him justice. "It's always a very handsome lad, but never me," he joked.

Tischbein, on the other hand, painted him well, during excursions in the Roman countryside, but found the painting too big for the Via del Corso lodgings they shared.

On visits to Villa Farnesina and the Palazzo Barberini—"to see Raphael's mistress painted by that great artist"—Kauffman shared with Goethe her knowledge of art. In edifying company, in an edifying city, the personal transformation and creative rekindling Goethe underwent in Rome, was almost epiphanous. "I count the day when I entered Rome as my second natal day, a true rebirth," he maintained ardently.

Having dabbled with the idea of becoming a painter, he realized he was born to write. Though he had written little in Rome, brushing against such greatness had helped ready him for his famous poetic drama *Faust*, penned

Self Portrait Angelica Kauffmann,
1780, Bündner Kunstmuseum,
Switzerland

between 1808-32, in the latter decades of his life.

After returning to Germany in June 1788, Rome stayed with Goethe.

The magnitude of his appreciation for his journey was expressed in *The Roman Elegies*, in 1793 and again in *Italienishce Reise*, a series of memories of his two-year voyage published as a series from 1816. Rome also allowed Goethe a new start sentimentally, though his marriage with Christiane Vulpius came a full two decades after their meeting and romance in Rome.

Despite being back in gloomy northern Europe, he was "happily inspired now on Classical soil."

Goethe felt so content after his trip to Rome, he wrote that he would even be content to die: "For the first time I achieved inner harmony and became happy and rational."

Under the city's spell, the great writer found himself.

Watching the full moon over Capitol Hill on the eve of his departure, he felt "transported into another simpler and greater world."

CAFFÈ GRECCO

Since the Caffè Grecco opened in 1760, great artists, philosophers, musicians and heads of state have dallied there, from Louis of Bavaria and Arthur Schopenhauer, to Felix Mendelssohn, Franz Liszt, Richard Wagner, Lord Byron, Charles Baudelaire, Stendhal and Orson Welles. The literary tradition at Caffè Greco today is more than nostalgic—it is still a serious rendezvous for writers, as well as espresso enthusiasts. .

CHAPTER 26

ROMANCING ROME: KEATS AND THE GHETTO INGELSI

1821

In the early 19th century, youthful British poets and artists visited Rome in droves, their imaginations fired by readings of Italian literature. Many belonged to the dreamy, expressive age of Romanticism, and were engaged in five decades of social and intellectual change between the French Revolution in 1789 and coronation of Queen Victoria in 1837.

English travelers colonized the area around the Piazza di Spagna, earning it the nickname Ghetto degli Inglesi, the English Ghetto. It was here, one of Britain's greatest poets, 25-year-old John Keats, died tragically of pulmonary tuberculosis in 1821. His memory will linger for eternity about the Spanish Steps—as that of a brilliant, but ill-fated young poet, in a devastatingly dreamy city.

Keats had set sail for Italy in September 1820, accompanied by his artist friend, Joseph Severn, already preyed on by the chronic consumption that had claimed both his mother and brother. It was the poet Percy Bysshe Shelley who urged him towards Italy's salutary climate, inviting him to his home in Pisa. Keats's publisher intervened and organized a trip to Rome.

Portrait of John Keats, by Joseph Severn, 1819, National Portrait Gallery, London

Born in London in 1795, Keats began his career as an apothecary surgeon. He abandoned that to concentrate on poetry, and had already completed two volumes by the time he left for Italy.

He was not just leaving England behind. In Hampstead, he had fallen desperately in love with the girl next door, Fanny Brawne, penning his masterpiece, "Ode to a Nightingale", in the garden between tormented love letters, in which he described himself

Self-portrait by Joseph Severn, age 29

as a "poor prisoner" of his unrequited passions.

Arriving in Naples, on October 21, he ended a letter to his sweetheart's mother, with "Good bye Fanny! God bless you." He could no longer tolerate the pain of writing to her, nor reading her letters, knowing that he was doomed.

"The persuasion that I shall see her no more will kill me...I can bear to die—I cannot bear to leave her," he wrote in a heart-rending letter to his friend, Charles Brown.

Once in Rome, Keats and Severn took lodgings in a pensione on the second floor of the Casina Rossa, the "little red house", at 26 Piazza di Spagna. His bedroom overlooked the Fontana della Barcaccia—the "useless old boat" fountain—by Bernini's father, Pietro. The house was built in 1725, in the same period that architect Francesco De Sanctis designed the scalinata di Trinità dei Monti, the Spanish Steps.

By the late 19th century, English Romantics flocked here, occupying most rooms in the *palazzetti* (small buildings) lining the stairs.

Keats, like his compatriots Shelley and Lord Byron, reveled in the sensations and sentiments stirred by Rome's worldly beauty, while 14th-century Italian writers such as Dante Alighieri helped unleash their libertarian spirits.

Left: View of the Piazza di Spagna, by Giovanni Battista Piranesi (1720-1778);
Right: The Casina Rossa, 26 Piazza di Spagna (Keats-Shelly House)

"The bright blue sky of Rome, and the effect of the vigorous awakening spring in that divinest climate, and the new life with which it drenches the spirits even to intoxication, were the inspiration of this drama," Shelley wrote in the preface to *Prometheus Unbound*, completed during a *soggiorno* in Rome in 1819.

Keats was robbed any such chance of new beginnings in Rome. After a massive lung hemorrhage on December 10, he never saw light of day again, except from his bedroom window.

Severn selflessly stayed by Keats's side for over two months, reading to him and redecorating the floral coffered ceiling of the poet's bedroom so he could spend his last days tiptoeing through imaginary tulips.

"I feel the flowers growing over me already," Keats uttered, after the bucolic Protestant Cemetery in which he was to be buried was described to him.

One morning at 3 a.m., to stop himself falling asleep, Severn sketched Keats, his hair drizzled limply down his forehead in "deadly sweat", head propped against a pillow like a sculpture, and finely carved features surrendering to closed, exhausted eyes.

Keats died at 11 p.m. on February 23, 1821, riddled with physical and emotional grief; not only had he loved so deeply and lost, but recent harsh critics of his work had led him to feel he was a failure.

*Portrait of Keats on His Death Bed,
From a Drawing by Joseph Severn,*
Reproduced 1895

"How long is this posthumous existence of mine to go on?" he had exclaimed in agony, shortly before his death, after his doctor refused him the laudanum he had smuggled to Rome.

Keats's torment endures in the epitaph on his tombstone: This grave contains all that was mortal of a young English poet, who on his death-bed in the bitterness of his heart at the malicious power of his enemies, desired these words to be engraved on his tomb stone. Here lies one whose name was writ in water.

Insisting no name or date appear on the inscription, Keats decided at the last minute, that an unread letter from Fanny—the very sight of which "tore him to pieces"—would not accompany him to the grave.

Hearing of his friend's death, Shelley wrote *Adonais*, his elegy to Keats, blaming his friend's sudden decline in the preface to the "savage criticism on his poems."

In an equally ardent manner, he describes Keats's resting place under the daisy- and violet-covered ruins of the Pyramid of Cestius, an Augustan-era tomb: "It might make one in love with death, to...[be] buried in so sweet a place."

Within thirteen months, Shelley too was dead, after a boating accident in July 1822. His badly maimed body, washed ashore, was identified by the book of Keats's poetry in pocket.

In a poignant tale of intertwined fates, Shelley was buried a few yards from Keats, and alongside the tomb of his 3-year old son William, who died from malaria in Rome in 1819.

Rome from Monte Testaccio, by Joseph Mallord William Turner, c. 1818

Half the second generation of English Romantic poets had been wiped out within a year, succumbing to wretched deaths in a country that promised creative fruition. The deaths of Shelley and Keats hold an aura of hallowed mystery, of the young genius, so tragically nipped in the bud in a foreign land.

Keats's death was all the less obscure, thanks to the letters of his devoted companion, Severn, who died at the ripe old age of 85 after serving several years as British Consul in Rome. He was buried alongside Keats in the Cimitero degli Inglesi.

KEATS–SHELLEY HOUSE

For over a century, the residence where Keats spent his dying days has been a museum and library dedicated to the Romantic poets and literature.

In 1903, American editor Robert Underwood Johnston began mustering up support among writers and diplomats to save the dilapidated building and turn it into the Keats-Shelley House.

The main wood-paneled *salone*, converted from the three small rooms which Keats and Severn once inhabited, displays manuscripts, letters and paintings, as well as several oddities: locks of John Milton's hair, Byron's wax carnival max, an urn containing a fragment of Shelley's jaw and Keats's death mask.

Tosca

CHAPTER 27.

TOSCA: ROME IN THREE ACTS
1900

The most famous theatrical work ever to put Rome at center stage, Giacomo Puccini's opera *Tosca* sets a psychological thriller of jealousy, betrayal and ill-fated love against the volatile political backdrop of Rome at the end of the 18th century. Its protagonists are embroiled in the era of the Napoleonic Wars and violent repression against anti-monarchist, Republican sympathizers.

The composer went to great lengths to bring the historical atmosphere alive, by casting the main settings—the Tiber-side Castel Sant'Angelo, Church of Sant'Andrea della Valle, and Palazzo Farnese—in the most accurate possible light. The final act of *Tosca* opens with the bells pealing around the theatrically charged Castel Sant'Angelo over the dawn-lit city. No other location in Rome could capture so potently the eerie despair of the play's climax.

In *Tosca*, Puccini was dealing with actual events and characters, and he wanted to create a sense of real-time storytelling, *verismo*.

His interest in the opera was kindled on seeing the play *La Tosca*, by Frenchman Victorien Sardou, in Milan in 1887. Sarah Bernhardt was cast in the lead role of celebrated soprano singer, Floria Tosca, which only added to the story's seduction for Puccini.

At barely 30, he was already an accomplished composer, and in the midst of writing his lyrical masterpiece *La Bohème* (which premiered in Turin in 1896).

Giacomo Puccini, c. 1908

Two years later, he wrote to his musical publisher, Giulio Ricordi, expressing his enthusiasm for getting the rights to the play. He also made clear his desire to achieve high historical fidelity in *Tosca*, "to get the who, what, and where right".

In this respect, he said, *Tosca* was very different from *La Bohème*, "where the facts are not important."

Location was vital for conveying historical atmosphere—and his approach did not fully coincide with the playwright's.

Visiting Sardou in Paris, in the process of getting the green light for his opera, Puccini admired the Frenchman's energetic intensity, but was alarmed at his insouciance with topographical accuracy. "I told him that the river flowed on the other side (of the fortress)…but he, calm as a fish, retorted, 'Oh that's nothing!'" Puccini famously remarked of "the strange man".

For Puccini, there was to be no such disregard of the real Rome. Born in Lucca, Tuscany, Puccini often visited Rome to see operas and knew the city well. He had his set designer Adolfo Hohenstein work from photos of the actual settings.

While planning the third act of *Tosca*, Puccini sat on the castle ramparts, listening to the chorus of morning bells from all the surrounding churches, and meticulously noting their tones. He then organized for a Roman poet,

Left: Stage photograph of the "Te Deum" scene in Act 1 of Puccini's 1900 opera *Tosca*;
Right: Basilica of Sant'Andrea della Valle

Luigi Zanazzo, to write the accompanying shepherd boy's song "*Io de'*
sospiri" in Roman dialect. By doing so, the play brought alive the semi-rural
atmosphere of Rome in 1800, as a backdrop for the turbulent events which
unfold in a 24-hour period from June 17 to June 18.

The opera opens with fugitive political prisoner, Angelotti, hiding in the
church of Sant'Andrea della Valle, where Floria Tosca's lover, the Bonaparte
partisan Mario Cavaradossi is painting. The sacristan brings "glorious news"
that Napoleon is being thrashed by the Austrians at the Battle of Marengo,
which took place in northern Italy in June 1800.

In pursuit of realism, Puccini switched churches, finding the play's original
setting, Bernini's Sant'Andrea al Quirinale, behind the presidential palace,
too remote from the Castel Sant'Angelo to allow for convincing prisoner
escape. Instead, he set the action in the giant-domed basilica, Sant'Andrea
della Valle, on the Corso Vittorio Emanuele II.

As the church fills for the Latin hymn, "*Te Deum*", the corrupt chief
of police, Baron Scarpia, resolves to kill Cavaradossi and possess the
jealous Tosca.

Tosca's political intrigue unravels in the second act, at the Palazzo Farnese,
whose symmetrical Renaissance façade and rows of gabled windows loom

*View of the Tiber Looking Towards the Castel Sant'Angelo, with Saint Peter's in the
Distance*, Giuseppe Zocchi, c. 1721-67, Private Collection

over the piazza of the same name. As Tosca performs a victorious *cantata*
in its riverside gardens, with Scarpia listening from his offices overhead, we
learn of Napoleon's victory, and it is Cavaradossi's time to celebrate.

At the time the play is set, Italian radicals saw in Napoleon freedom from
the tyranny of the old regime, in which Rome was almost a police state,
ruled by a pope-king on behalf of the Naples-based monarchy.

In 1799, the French were forced to abandon their short-lived republic in
Rome, allowing the pope to return to sovereignty. Ironically, the Farnese has
been owned and occupied by the French Embassy since 1874.

As Cavaradossi is tortured, and led away for execution, Scarpia—"a
thoroughly corrupt figure who claims to be working in the name of the
Church while actually serving his own completely godless agenda",
according to one director—tricks Tosca into thinking he will spare her lover
if she gives herself to him.

The melodramatic story of cruelty and vengeance, climaxes in Act II with
Tosca lamenting her cruel fate in the aria, *"Vissi d'arte, vissi d'amore"* ("I
lived for art, I lived for love.")

The play winds up at the Castel St'Angelo at dawn, where Cavaradossi is

Teatro Costanzi (Teatro dell'Opera), c. 1926-28

imprisoned. Tricked into believing her lover will be released, Tosca kills Scarpia. When she discovers Cavaradossi is actually dead, she throws herself from the castle's ramparts declaring *"O Scarpia, avanti a Dio!"* (O Scarpia, we shall meet before God).

The curtains first rose on *Tosca*, at the Teatro Constanzi in Rome, in January 1900 — in a politically charged city. With peak Holy Year celebrations underway, the operas scenes of torture, sadism and suicide — and its anti-clerical themes — clashed with the upsurge of religious faith.

Despite nervousness among the cast, and bomb threats, *Tosca* went off with a bang, and has done so ever since.

The "shabby little shocker" with "second-rate" music, as American musicologist Joseph Kernan described the play in 1956, has been widely praised for its realistic rendition of Rome, and just as Puccini wished, and for underscoring the naked facts, with passionate, and powerfully stirring music."

By capturing Rome at a certain time and place, *Tosca* embedded itself in the cultural landscape of the Eternal City. As the Italian jingle for the opera continues to claim: *"Tosca*: from the real places, at the real times."

CHAPTER 28

RUINING ROME: MUSSOLINI'S ROAD THROUGH IMPERIAL HISTORY

1930s

Just as the Roman Empire fell slowly but surely, a victim of its own success, ancient Rome has fallen bit by precious bit, prey to ignorance, plundering, natural disaster, dodgy digs and reckless urban planning.

The most recent and dramatic destruction of Rome's critical mass of antiquity came in the 1930s when Italy's fascist dictator Benito Mussolini (whose admirers included Adolf Hitler), ordered the building of a major road through the heart of historic Rome. The Via dei Fori Imperiali was ironically named after the precious assembly of emperors' forums it tore apart.

The wonder of Rome is that its ruins, even those in a threadbare state, are somehow alive—a stony anachronism surging up amid the eternal chaos of modern life and mobile phones. Today the remains of the private forums of Caesar, Vespasian, Augustus, Nerva and Trajan, built between 46 B.C. and 112 A.D., are scattered opposite those of the Roman Forum, the mother of all forums and meeting place of the Senate.

The imperial *fora* were hubs of political, religious, and judicial life. Each of the emperors had one. Following on the model of the Forum Augustum, they

Illustration, *Mussolini with a Pickaxe* on the Cover of *La Domenica del Corriere*, 1936

contained" law courts, temples, colonnades and basilicas. The imperial addiction to supersizing culminated with the last such structure, the Forum of Trajan—neighboring his triumphant sphinx-like column and immense, semicircular market.

Crossing between the two clusters of forum ruins, you will struggle to make your way through the traffic blight, which rips a mighty hole into what could be a peaceful stroll through Roman relics—and a literal one into Roman antiquity. Get your bearings, and you will find yourself hovering over the vast excavated pits of two-thousand-year-old remains, alongside the Via dei Fiori Imperiali.

Such major urban thoroughfares usually signal they are going somewhere— that they will lead you to the place of their namesake. In this case, the Via dei Fori Imperiali cuts carelessly right through the heart of the prized sites from which it takes its name.

During the Fascist-era renovations of the early 1930s, Mussolini set his signs on creating a ceremonial boulevard, connecting the National Fascist Party headquarters in Piazza Venezia with the Colosseum, via the seat of ancient Roman power in the Forum, with which he strongly identified.

"Rome must appear in all its splendor: immense, ordered, and as powerful as it was at the time of the first empire, that of Augustus," *Il Duce* declared.

Mussolini's strong identification with idealistic rulers of ancient Rome, particularly Augustus, is widely acknowledged, as is his association with other historical patriots, like the 14th-century people's tribune, Cola di Rienzo. On the bi-millennial of Augustus's birth in 1937, Mussolini commissioned a reconstruction of the *Ara Pacis*, the 2,000-year-old Altar of Peace, inaugurated by the Roman Senate in 9 B.C. to honor Augustus on his return from wars in Spain and Gaul.

The "Fascist route" through Rome was built after extensive excavations of the Forum starting in 1931, and launched the next year, with Mussolini riding down it on horseback. Photos of the excavations look like a war zone, in which one of the city's vital historic ensembles was dismembered for a mundane four-lane street. The original name, Via dell'Impero, rightly linked the blight of the "Emperor" Mussolini.

In his sweeping renovation program, Mussolini sought to rid Rome of its ancient clutter, to "liberate the trunk of the great oak from everything which still smothers it," he declared in 1925. "Everything which has grown up in the centuries of decadence must be swept away."

Landmarks deemed inconsequential by Mussolini and his team were removed, many of them long-standing marvels. The road decimated nearly 85 percent of the recently excavated forums of Nerva and Trajan, and led to partial obliteration of the others, along with swathes of medieval and Renaissance history.

Dozens of treasures were demolished, displaced or forever buried during the birth of the road: 16th- and 17th-century churches, convents, noble *domus*, gardened sanctuaries, *nymphaeums* and an entire working-class neighborhood.

Later, the name Via dei Fori Imperiali was given to Mussolini's road, as though trying to recall up things which had been eternally lost.

While his public works program—and the nation-exalting ideology underpinning it—had won Mussolini many fans, his appeal wore off by the 1940s. Fed up with his megalomaniacal behavior, a failing economy, and his alliance with Nazi Germany, he and his mistress, Clara Petacci, were killed near Como in northern Italy, in 1943, while fleeing Allied forces.

Demolition for Via dei Fori Imperiali, c. 1932-33

Though official accounts say Mussolini was executed by Italian anti-Fascist
resistance movement partisan Walter Audisio, in the name of the Italian
people, speculation about his final hours include claims of British secret
service involvement in his death.

No such doubts existed over the Italian public's view of their slain leader.
Taken to Milan, his body was strung upside down alongside that of
his mistress, from the rafters of a gas station in Piazzale Loreto. Angry
civilians spat at, stoned and trampled on the bodies—in a vivid symbol
of the death of fascism and a potent warning to anyone who tried follow
in *Il Duce*'s footsteps.

Via dei Fori Imperial (left) and Roman Forum (right) today.

ROME'S FASCIST ARCHITECTURE

Mussolini displayed ambivalence towards Roman archaeological heritage, superciliously trashing the achievements of the emperors, yet appropriating their personality-cult constructions. After contemptuously ripping up the work of the ancients, under his vision *urbanista*, *Il Duce* was planning a modernist take on ancient Rome in the suburbs.

The Fascist dictator tried to out-ego his role model, Emperor Augustus, by adding his own monumental buildings to the city silhouette. In 1937, construction began on his Fascist wonderland, five miles south of the city, with the goal of showing off the precinct at the Esposizione Universale di Roma in 1942, the international exhibition that was cancelled due to WWII.

Filled with colossal Neoclassical takes on ancient buildings, the "EUR" had its very own obelisk; a forum, the Foro Italico; and "Square Colosseum", the Palazzo della Civiltà del Lavoro.

The stark Fascist buildings, wide avenues and grassy expanses are today a commercial and government district centered on the Piazza Guglielmo Marconi, formerly the Piazza Imperiale.

CHAPTER 29.

ROMAN HOLIDAY: AUDREY HEPBURN IN ROME

1953

With her first major starring role, as Princess Anne in *Roman Holiday*, Audrey Hepburn began a lifelong love affair with Rome. Like the film, a big chunk of the British starlet's life was "lived, loved and filmed in Rome."

Hepburn was 24, when she shot her Oscar-winning performance as the rebellious young princess in 1953. The fêted actress, style icon and humanitarian ambassador was destined to spend another three decades of filming and family life in the city.

Hepburn's final lines as the perky princess on a goodwill tour of European capitals, were strangely prophetic of a deep personal connection she would develop with Rome. "Which of the cities visited did Your Highness enjoy the most?" a journalist asks as she addresses the press in the famous final scene, filmed in the gold and marble filled Sala Grande of the Palazzo Colonna

"Each, in its own way was, unforgettable…Rome; by all means, Rome. I will cherish my visit here, in memory, as long as I live," she says, having chosen duty over love. Her words mask her real reason of attachment to

Galleria Colonna

Rome: the love affair with Joe Bradley, the dashing reporter played by Gregory Peck, whom she is bidding *arrivederci*.

As Joe turns slowly towards the exit, the camera pans through the stucco columns of the 250-foot-long Great Hall of the 16th-century palace.

From that moment on, Hepburn's professional and private lives would increasingly bind her to Rome.

With just a few films and TV series behind her, Hepburn shot to sudden stardom with *Roman Holiday*. The success brought heavy new personal demands, from which there would be no return, until she retired from acting.

In Rome, the paparazzi and fans mobbed her from the time she stepped off the plane to begin filming. Promoted as a "fast travelogue", the original film trailer shows Hepburn, as Princess Anne, speeding out of control through Rome on a Vespa, giving Joe "the royal run around."

"A Princess Goes on a Spree" was the title of *Life* magazine's Movie of the Week article in August 1953, as the film opened. The story shows photos of the two stars whizzing around the city, pursued by the paparazzi.

After the initial encounter between Joe and the princess at the Roman Forum, the itinerant film crisscrosses Rome, and dozens of its iconic locations: a haircut near the Trevi Fountain; Joe Bradley's apartment at Via Margutta 51 in the heart of the historic center; a rendezvous on the Spanish Steps; a café on the Piazza della Rotonda near the Pantheon; and a night of dancing on a barge on the Tiber.

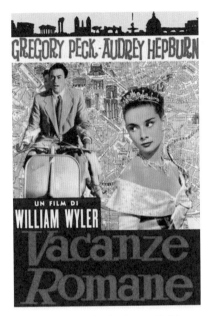

Italian movie poster for *Roman Holiday*

"Where do you live?" Asks Joe Bradley, spotting the Princess at the Forum. "Colosseum," an inebriated Princess Anne replies, mumbling under the influence of sleeping tablets that were intended to keep her indoors at night.

"She lives in the Colosseum," he declares to the taxi driver. "Is wrong address!" the startled driver replies.

The Princess's embassy in Rome was in fact the Palazzo Barberini, at least for exterior shots.

Interior shots—the reception ball in her honor and the quarters from which she escaped—were filmed at the Palazzo Brancaccio on Viale del Monte Oppio, near Nero's old digs on the Oppio Hill.

The last of Rome's patrician palaces, the palace was built in 1880 for Prince Salvatore Brancaccio. His American wife, the "Principessa" Mary Elisabeth Field, held grand, stately bashes in its banquet rooms for the King Umberto di Savoia.

Gazing into the Brancaccio's magnificent grounds, and onto a crowded garden party, Hepburn's filmic princess longed to free herself from her duties—which she does, in the back of a delivery truck.

Possibly the film's most hilarious scene happens at the Bocca della Verità. Legend holds that the "mouth of the truth"—a stone dial with hollowed out eyes and woolly hair—will bite off the hand of a liar. After goading Anne to try first, Joe puts his hand into the sculpture's open mouth, and feigns an attack by the creature.

La Bocca della Vertia

Located inside the portico entrance of the Tiber-side Basilica di Santa Maria in Cosmedin, on the Piazza della Bocca della Verità, the figure may be an ancient drain cover, or part of a fountain, dating to the 1st century.

Despite the stifling heat, and political tensions in Rome at the time, Audrey looked like she was enjoying the same freedom on location as her princess character.

The romantic comedy was shot in the summer of 1952, as fascists and communists confronted each other in the streets; explosives were found near one of the locations by the Tiber.

Far from letting the success of the film go to her head, the international proclaim she won with *Roman Holiday* did little to boost Hepburn's self-esteem…"she was basically an insecure person whose insecurity made everyone fall in love with her," her eldest son Sean once wrote. For most of her life, he said, she was "a star who couldn't see her own light.'"

"I probably hold the distinction of being one movie star who, by all laws of logic, should never have made it," Hepburn herself once declared. "At each stage of my career I lacked the experience. But at least I never pretended to be able to do the things that were being offered."

The film proved a major turning point in her destiny with Rome. Returning to London for the premiere, she met her first husband, Mel Ferrer, at a party. The actor-director was a close friend of co-star Gregory Peck.

In 1955, *Life* magazine showed the newlyweds enjoying a holiday in the Roman countryside during filming of *War and Peace*.

That marriage did not last, but it, along with her subsequent, 13-year marriage to Italian psychiatrist Andrea Dotti, produced an intrinsic, life-long tie with the city: her two children, Sean Ferrer and Luca Dotti.

In the early 1970s she enjoyed setting up home with Dotti near the Corso Vittorio Emanuele and later in the elegant Parioli district near Villa Borghese, with penthouse views over Rome. "I am a Roman housewife," she declared. Signora Andrea Dotti, as the American press called her, came to truly feel at home in Rome, and lived life like a Roman, shopping, meeting friends for lunch, going to the theater and museums.

According to her younger son, Luca Dotti, his mother loved to walk "like an everyday woman," through the squares and streets of Rome, and mingle with the public. "She spent nearly thirty years of her life in this city, and was known to locals—shopkeepers, bookbinders, framers and the taxi drivers," said Luca, one of the curators of the 2011 exhibition, "Audrey a Roma." Through archival news material, the retrospective showed many "stolen moments" of Hepburn's years in Rome, out and about, garbed elegantly in Givenchy suits or Burberry trench coat.

The actress was often seen strolling the streets of Rome: shopping with Luca; with her husband Andrea Dotti, in box seats at the theater; before the wolf statue at the Musei Capitolini; disembarking at Ciampino and returning home to Rome, the city in which she lived, worked, married, and raised her children.

Movie poster for *War and Peace*

Luca Dotti said his mother found freedom in Rome's *fa niente* attitude and laid-back ways: "An early riser, she loved to go shopping on her own in Rome's *botteghe*, thanks to the city's certain air of indolence, which comforted her, and left her to enjoy her own time and space."

They were also troubled years. An intensely private Hepburn did not warm to Dotti's wooing of journalists to their doorstep, nor to his blatant infidelity. "Italian husbands have never been famous for being faithful," he said, after their divorce in 1981.

Even on her permanent move to her Swiss hideaway in the mid 1980s — where she lived with her companion, the Dutch actor Robert Wolders, until her death from appendix cancer in 1993 — Rome's *dolce vita*, and the spontaneous residents, left a lasting impression on Hepburn.

During the shooting of *War and Peace* in 1956, producer Dino De Laurentiis spent an evening with Hepburn and his actress-wife, Silvana Mangano.

In his biography *Dino: The Life & Films of Dino de Laurentiis*, the director recounted how the actress, under Rome's influence, let her hair down, just like her character in *Roman Holiday*, Princess Anne:

"Audrey felt a strong empathy for Italians, for their warmth, their exuberant and slightly crazy humor, their energy, their fits of bad temper, laughter and tears. Always so controlled herself, she loved and envied their lack of control."

PALAZZO COLONNA

Palazzo Colonna, 1748

A fortress and family residence for a string of popes and cardinals from the powerful Colonna clan since the Middle Ages, the Palazzo Colonna overlooks Piazza dei Santa Apostoli. The soaring ceiling fresco of its Great Hall fêtes Marcantonio Colonna's 1571 victory for papal forces in the Battle of Lepanto.

Several rooms of the palace's Baroque wing showcase the Colonna collection of 15th- to 17th-century paintings, including dramatic religious and mythological scenes by Jacopo Tintoretto, French artist Nicolas Poussin and the Venetian Paolo Veronese.

CHAPTER 30.

THE TREVI FOUNTAIN: ANITA EKBERG, FELLINI & LA DOLCE VITA

1960

It is one of the most compelling moments in cinematic history: a triumph of gloriously sculpted white travertine stone, towering sea gods and writhing stallions, colliding with a modern goddess of ivory flesh and heavenly hourglass proportions. In the legendary Trevi Fountain scene of the 1960s classic, *La Dolce Vita*, the statuesque Swedish sex bomb Anita Ekberg, in the role of Sylvia, wades through the water in a strapless black dress, her voluptuous breasts framed by a sensuous blonde mane. The episode clings to the collective memory of the Baroque fountain, which like Ekberg, is a work of abundant curves.

Director Federico Fellini chose the larger-than-life Scandinavian beauty as a symbol of Italy's post-war "economic miracle", a period of prosperity in which excessive materialism and decadence fostered meaninglessness and cynicism.

Ekberg's powerful presence matched the strong emotions he had for his adopted city.

"Rome became my home as soon as I saw it. I was born that moment," he declared, after arriving there from the coastal city of Rimini in 1938.

Opposite Ekberg, Fellini cast Marcello Mastroianni as Marcello Rubini, whose character captures the era's disillusionment and moral weakness with *triste* irony. Abandoning his literary ambitions for a career as a gossip columnist, the handsome Marcello wiles away his time with Rome's debauched glamour set of actors and aristocrats, the nouveau rich and social climbers.

Director Federico Fellini

In real life, the actor's constitution was apparently no match for the statuesque Swede.

To capture the iconic Trevi Fountain scene, Ekberg withstood the cold March night and freezing spring waters for hours, while Mastroianni not only required a wetsuit beneath his clothes, but warmed himself up by downing copious amounts of vodka. "I was half-drunk with vodka by the time we got finished with a night's shooting," he later told biographers.

Like many Rome locations, the Trevi is a natural stage, prone to incite dream-like qualities in the observer, by the sheer weight of its cascading beauty and history. Add to that Fellini's manner of mixing dreams with reality, and the scene becomes intensely surreal.

Already a luminary with Oscars for both *La Strada* and *Nights of Cabiria*, Fellini went from art house to a wider audience with *La Dolce Vita*, and introduced the terms paparazzi, the "sweet life" and Felliniesque (referring to the director's quirky, surrealistic style) into the English language.

Ekberg, who famously declared, "It was I who made Fellini famous," was prey to the diva-hunting paparazzi scourge from the moment she set foot in Rome. Her meeting with Fellini and casting in the film was a complete coincidence. Arriving in Rome in 1955 to film *War and Peace*, she lived

The Trevi Fountain

with her husband Anthony Steel at the Hôtel de Ville on Trinita dei Monti, and drove her Mercedes 300 SL convertible every day to the Cinecittà studio. Ekberg's exuberant womanliness must have fitted with Fellini's view of Rome as "a completely feminine city."

Fellini was also bowled over by Ekberg's physical assets and began "badgering her to appear in the film," says Fellini biographer John Baxter.

The actress knew where the source of her real talents lay. "I had only long blonde hair and a magnificent bosom, but the 'sweet life' was like a walk for me, I could do it blindfolded."

In her first discussions with Fellini about the film, she was frustrated by her role, or rather lack of it. "He refused to show her a script because one didn't really exist," says Baxter, "and he couldn't explain the role of Sylvia Rank, since he didn't know what it would be. In fact, Sylvia doesn't exist as a character at all."

"This is a joke. This is crazy," Ekberg told her agent. "I cannot make a film with a madman like that." But her agent had signed the contract and she was stuck.

The late night dip at the Trevi was take two for Ekberg. Before she met Fellini, she had acted the whole thing out spontaneously, with her photographer friend Pierluigi. Wandering about on a midsummer's night barefoot, she cut her foot, and went in search of a fountain in which to bathe it.

Stumbling upon the Piazza di Trevi, Pierluigi began to shoot, and the photos "went like hot cakes."

"I wore a dress of white cotton and pink shirt...I pulled up the skirt and was immersed in the bath, saying to Pierluigi: 'You cannot imagine how this water is fresh, you come too.'"

Having thrown more than a coin in the Trevi Fountain, Ekberg not only returned to Rome, she has been captured forever, in an image as eternal as the city itself.

THE VIA VENETO

La Dolce Vita had a bitter side. The film satirizes the debauchery and moral decay of Rome in the 1960s, amid the glitzy café society of cinéastes, starlets, gossip columnists, playboys and paparazzi who swarmed about the Via Veneto—officially the via Vittorio Veneto. Fellini heightened the charade, by scattering real-life celebrities among the cast and mixing dream-like sequences with actual events.

"Think of it as a kind of fictionalized newsreel," says Fellini biographer John Baxter. "Fellini incorporated the latest scandals into the script as it evolved over several months. The orgy and Nadia Gray's strip, for example, were inspired by the Montesi case, in which the partly-clothed body of a working-class girl was found dead at the beach, assumed to have died at a party in a nearby villa."

The murder of Wilma Montesi, in 1953, marked the actual start of the "*dolce vita*", according to a chronicler of the day. In his book *La Dolce*

Via Veneto

Vita, Minute by Minute, journalist Victor Ciuffa tells how he inspired Fellini to create the Mastroianni role by sharing spicy tales and tidbits with him at the Café de Paris, on Via Veneto.

Prowling about day and night, among "existentialist-imitating artists", "actors who were flocking to Rome because Hollywood had moved there", and "aristocrats in search of excitement", Ciuffa says his path crossed with Fellini and his screenwriter friends such as Ennio Flaiano, sitting at the landmark café. His stories of corrupt, drug-abusing and love-struck aristocrats pleased Fellini, because they were always "seasoned with irony and a pinch of satire."

These were the days, writes Tullio Kezich, in *Federico Fellini: His Life and His Work*, when the caffè—Rosati, Doney and Strega-Zeppa—were frequented by famous intellectuals and journalists. They were places to eavesdrop, "on the most current conversations, witty punning and polemics about culture." With the death of Pope Pius XII in October 1958, came an "explosion of a sort of street party that will rage for several years on via Veneto." The media and entertainment world in particular reveled in long nights on the brightly lit street.

By 1963, says Ciuffa, the economic decline had begun, and the bubble burst on the sweet life of cafés and nightclubs. "*La Dolce Vita* does not start, but dies with Fellini's film."

Scandalous in its day, particularly in Vatican circles, Fellini and his film were accused of representing Rome as vice-filled city. *La Dolce Vita* earned posthumous fame, after Fellini's death in 1994, while the via Veneto, with its swanky lineup of nightclubs, luxury hotels and cafés, has become a hotbed location, if not for the *literati*, for tourists.

ROME
WALKING TOURS

3

Sant'Angelo

Vatican City

4

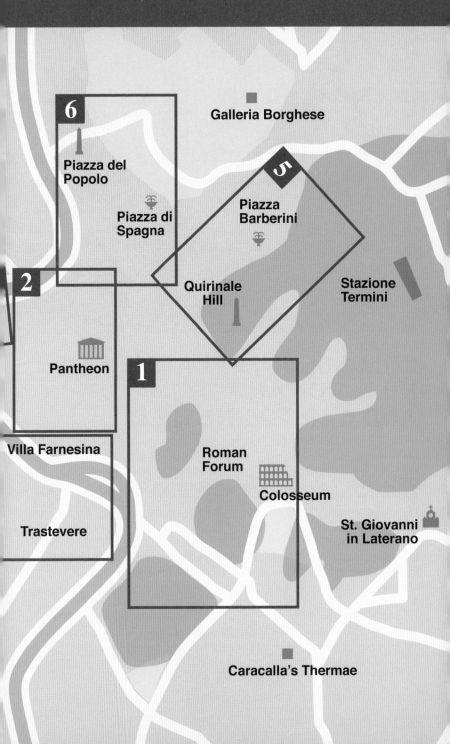

6

Piazza del
Popolo

♒

Piazza di
Spagna

2

🏛
Pantheon

Galleria Borghese ■

5

Piazza
Barberini

♒

Quirinale
Hill

Stazione
Termini

1

Roman
Forum

🏛
Colosseum

St. Giovanni
in Laterano ⛪

Villa Farnesina

Trastevere

Caracalla's Thermae ■

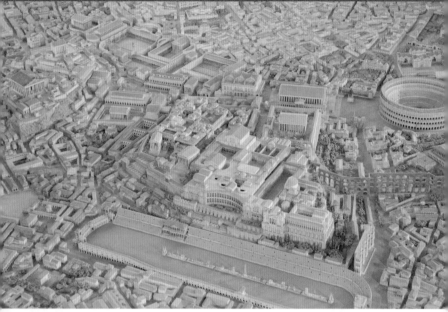

COLOSSEUM, PALATINE HILL, ROMAN FORUM AND CAPITOLINE HILL

1 Colosseum
2 Arch of Constantine
3 Aqua Claudia
4 Severan Complex
5 Palatine Stadium
6 Domus Augustana
7 The Domus Flavia
8 Cryptoporticus
9 Casa di Livia

10 Orti Farnesiani
11 Templum Veneris et Romae
12 Arch of Titus
13 Basilica of Maxentius
14 Temple of Caesar
15 Curia Julia
16 Piazza del Campidoglio
17 Cordonata of the Capitoline Hill
18 Via dei Fori Imperiali

START:
The Colosseum: Metro,
Linea B to Colosseo

END:
Piazza Venezia: Bus 40
and 64 to Termini station

Tour Time:
About 4 hours

Chapters:
1, 3, 4, 7, 8, 14

The Vintage Festival (detail), by Lawrence Alma-Tadema, 1870

The ruins of ancient Rome's imperial palaces surround the summit and slopes of Rome's central hill, the Palatino, above the Roman Forum. Opposite, Rome's most famous landmark, the Colosseum, is hemmed in by the triumphal arches of Titus and Constantine. Some of Rome's earliest settlements existed on the Palatine around 800 B.C., and the Lupercal—a grotto linked to the legend of Romulus and Remus—lies below the hill. It is here where legend holds, Romulus founded Rome, and the Palatine was the center of Roman political and religious life from the time of the Roman kings. About a mile in circuit, its summit rises 140 feet above the Tiber.

1 On the Piazza del Colosseo, the gigantic gladiator's amphitheatre with its empty windows opening on the sky dominates the valley between the Palatine, Caelian and Oppian hills (Palatino, Celio and Oppio in Italian). Construction began with Emperor Vespasian in 70 A.D., and was completed a decade later by his son Titus. Upon completion, it was the largest sporting arena in ancient Rome, seating up to 80,000. A combined

ticket allows two-day entry to the Colosseo, Foro Romano, Palatino archeological ensemble, and any exhibitions and monuments within them.

Walk south along the Via di San Gregorio in front of the Colosseum. You will pass the visitors exit to the Palatine Hill on your right.

2 On your left is the triumphal Arch of Constantine, one of three remaining imperial arches in Rome, completed in 315 A.D. to celebrate Constantine's victory in the Battle of the Milvian Bridge, which paved his way to becoming emperor. Covered in statues and reliefs recycled from earlier monuments of Hadrian and Marcus Aurelius, the arch is 85 feet wide, 70 feet high and 23 feet deep.

Then & Now

The Flavian Amphitheatre (Colosseum), artist's reconstruction by Louis Duquet; detail at right

Colosseum and Arch of Constantine, by Bernardo Bellotto, c. 1742

The second gate on your right, a few hundred feet along the Via di San Gregorio, is the entry to the Palatino and Roman Forum complex.

From the entry, start climbing up the path on the Palatino slope. Here you will encounter ruins of the homes of the Roman emperors.

3 The first ruins you pass through are part of the Aqua Claudia. Flavian Emperor Domitian added this branch to Caligula's aqueduct in the first century, to serve the imperial palaces.

Near the top of the hill, signposts point to the Palatine's various sites. Be warned: It is a labyrinth, but major features are numbered on interpretation panels.

4 The Severan complex, the first hilltop site you come to, includes the Severan Arcades (*arcate*) and baths (*thermae*), built by Septimius in the 2nd century. The double row of brick *arcate*, over half a

FLAVIAN EMPERORS

The Flavian emperors ruled the Roman Empire between 69 and 96 A.D., encompassing the reigns of Vespasian (69–79), and his two sons Titus (79–81) and Domitian (81–96). The major event in the reign of Vespasian was the revolt of the Jews, which resulted in the destruction of Jerusalem. The reign of Titus was marred by multiple natural disasters, the most severe of which, the eruption of Mount Vesuvius in 79, left the surrounding cities of Pompeii and Herculaneum completely buried under ash and lava. One year later, Rome was struck by fire and a plague. For his part, Domitian strengthened the economy by revaluing the Roman coinage. Flavian rule came to an end on September 18, 96, when Domitian was assassinated by an angry mob (including members of the Praetorian Guard, household staff, his wife Domitia and members of Roman nobility) for his tyranny. Left: *The Triumph of Titus: The Flavians*, by Lawrence Alma-Tadema, 1885

Chariot race (Circus Maximus), by Jean Léon Gérôme, 1876, Domus Augustana shows top left

mile long and 45 feet high encloses the remains of the multi-level baths dating to 190 A.D. Excavations have revealed a vast underground system of boilers and pipes.

5 Extending the entire length of the imperial palace, the massive rectangular hippodrome is believed to be the work of the Emperor Domitian, built around 86 A.D. Invariably called the Palatine Stadium or Stadium of Domitian, the 520-foot-long, 160-foot-wide arena is scattered with vestiges of marble and granite columns. The crescent-shaped area at its southern end was a private spectator's box.

6 The stadium flanks the ruins of the emperors' private quarters, Domus Augustana, to the west. The lower level of the two-story residence was about 40 feet below ground. The upper floor had a large peristyle (or open) colonnade, ponds and a small temple to Minerva, the Roman goddess of wisdom. A vestibule led into the official imperial palace next door.

7 The importance of the imperial palaces on the Palatine, explains how palatine—*palatium* in Latin—led to the word palace. The Domus Flavia, built by Domitian in 92 A.D., had a basilica, large

Domus Augustana from Circus Maximus

Domus Augustana and Domus Flavia

Farnese Gardens, 1761

peristyle courtyard, summer dining *triclinium* and gardened *nymphaeum*. In the center of one wing was a vast hall decorated with alcoves and marble columns, where the emperor sat in a throne before his audience.

8 Today Tiberius's and Caligula's palaces are gone, while their lowest levels remain buried. The *cryptoporticus* underground passageway is still intact; it goes from the palace substructures to the Clivus Palatinus road and the Casa di Livia, home of Rome's first Empresses, Livia Drusilla, or Julia Augusta. In this corridor, Caligula may have been assassinated by members of the Praetorian Guard led by Cassius Chaerea on January 24, 41 A.D.

9 The cryptoporticus leads to the Casa di Livia, part of the Domus Augusti complex. These were relatively modest imperial homes of Emperor Augustus and his wife Livia, also known as Julia Augusta. For some time, the children of Livia's son Germanicus, including Caligula and Agrippina, were raised here.

10 Enjoy the sweeping views from the crumbled *terrazzi* of the Orti Farnesiani, the 15th-century gardens built on top of the Domus Tiberiana. Emperor Tiberius's residence dominated the northwest corner of the Palatine Hill, when it was built around 14 A.D. Its arched façade is visible in the hillside above the Roman Forum. Emperor Claudius lived here with his family, including third wife Valeria Messalina and his fourth and final wife, Agrippina the Younger, mother of Nero. Claudius was killed here, during a party, in 54.

Scattered through the small valley between the Palatine and Capitoline Hills are the breathtaking

View of the Foro Romano from Farnese Gardens

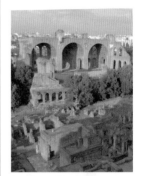

Basilica of Maxentius

vestiges of the Foro Romano, the central meeting place of ancient Rome. Its development from a marshland into Republican Rome's social, political, administrative and religious center happened bit by bit, but Julius Caesar and the first emperor, Augustus, sculpted its form. Extraordinary temples, shines and basilica were built, burned, restored and replaced, only to fall again. Today the major Republican-era remnants are the Curia Julia (Senate House) and foundations of the Basilica Julia. One of the Empire's main remnants is the ornately carved white marble Arch of Septimius Severus.

11 Head back towards the Colosseum. When you reach the Via Sacra, the main street of ancient Rome, which connected the Capitoline with the Roman Forum, turn left to reach the Forum. On the right, at Piazza Venere et Nova are ruins of Emperor Hadrian's Templum Veneris et Romae, partly built over by the Chiesa di Santa Maria Nova.

12 Pass by the Arch of Titus, which was built circa 82 A.D. to commemorate Emperor Titus's victories, including the Siege of Jerusalem in 70 A.D., to arrive at the Roman Forum.

View of the Arch of Titus, by Casper Andriaans van Wittel, c. 1710s

Basilica of Maxentius, 1890

Temple of Caesar, artist's reconstruction

13 As you walk towards the Capitoline Hill, note the arches of the Basilica of Maxentius, still standing after seventeen centuries. The frontal colonnades are all that remain of the Temple of Vespasian.

14 Located on the east side of the main square of the Forum near the Regia and the Temple of Vesta, the Temple of Caesar was built by Augustus in 29 B.C. On March 17, 44 B.C. Caesar's cremation was conducted on the place where the temple stood. Incensed at Mark Antony's funeral oration, a crowd interrupted the ceremony, demanding that Caesar's body be burned in Pompey's Curia, where he had been killed. Instead, they made an improvised funeral pyre from furniture, and burned his body in the middle of the Forum. Only the concrete core of the podium and a few marble fragments of the circular altar where Caesar was cremated remain.

15 The Senate House or Curia Julia stands on the right. Though it bears Caesar's name, it was still under construction when Caesar was murdered, and was completed by his adopted son, the Emperor Augustus.

Pass by the Arch of Septimius Severus and climb up Capitoline Hill. Pause at the top of the hill to catch the best sunset view over the Forum and the

Then & Now

Left: *View of Campo Vaccino (Forum)*, by Giovanni Battista Piranesi, 1756

Roman Forum, artist's reconstruction by Becchetti

Top: Artist's reconstruction of the Forum based on results of excavations and the written sources (The Basilica Julia, the Temple of Saturn, the Temple of Vespasian, the Temple of Concord, the Tabularium.); Bottom: *View of the Roman Forum after excavations*, by Ferdinand Dutert, 1874, L'École Nationale Supérieure des Beaux-Arts

The Temple of Jupiter Capitolinus (reconstruction drawing, J. Carlu, 1924)

The Marble Steps Leading to the Church of Santa Maria in Aracoeli, by C. W. Eckersberg, 1814-16

Colosseum, just like Matt Damon's character in the film *The Talented Mr. Ripley*.

16 The Capitoline Hill is the smallest of Rome's seven hills, but it was the religious and political center of the city since its foundation more than 2,500 years ago. In Ancient Rome the most important temple, the Temple of Jupiter Capitolinus was located on the hill.

The Piazza del Campidoglio at its top is home to various wings of the Musei Capitolini (Capitoline Museums): the Palazzo Senatorio, Palazzo dei Conservatori and Palazzo Nuovo. An equestrian statue of Marcus Aurelius stands the center of the square. It is a replica of the 2 A.D. original found inside the museum. Michelangelo redesigned the Piazza del Campidoglio and its new staircase, between 1536 and 1546, for Pope Paul III.

17 Decending the *cordonata*, or wide-ramped stairs, a statue of Cola di Rienzo stands on the right. In 1141 a revolt by Cola di Rienzo against the authority of the pope and nobles led to a senator taking up his official residence on the Capitoline Hill . On October 8th, 1354 he was dragged to the steps of the Capitoline Hill and stabbed to death.

18 At the end of the stair turn right to Piazza Venezia. The wide avenue leading to the Colosseum is the Via dei Fori Imperiali, constructed under Benito Mussolini.

HIGHLIGHTS FROM MUSEI CAPITOLINI

1. *Combat of the Horatii and the Curiatii*, by Cavalier d'Arpino, 1612-13 **2.** *Capitoline Venus*, by unknown, 96-192 **3.** *Rape of the Sabines*, by Pietro da Cortona, 1630-31 **4.** *Saint John the Baptist*, by Caravaggio, 1602 **5.** *Baptism of Christ*, by Tintoretto, 1585 **6.** Fragments of a colossal statue of Constantine, artist unknown, 300-400 **7.** *Capitoline Gaul*, artist unknown, 100-199

ANCIENT ROME MAPS FROM SAMUEL BALL PLATNER

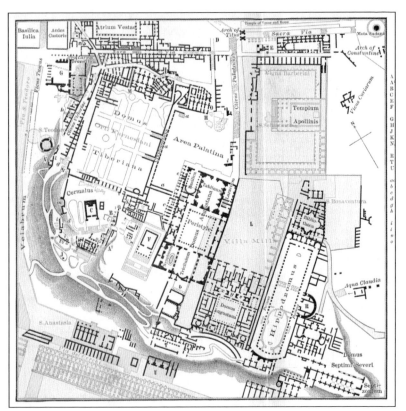

Palatine Hill

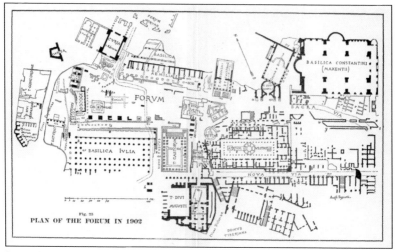

Roman Forum

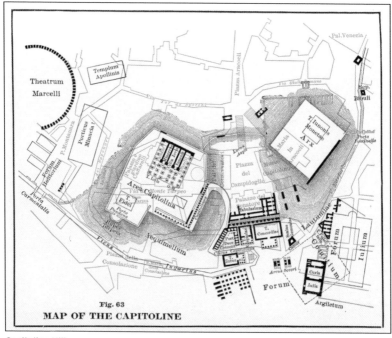

Capitoline Hill

THE COURSE OF EMPIRE

The Savage State, 1834

The Arcadian or Pastoral State, 1834

The Course of Empire is a five-part series of paintings created by American painter Thomas Cole between 1833 and 1836. Through images of the rise and fall of an imaginary city, Cole presents a cyclical view of history in which a civilization appears, matures and collapses.

Cole drew from a number of literary sources, such as Edward Gibbon's *The Decline and Fall of the Roman Empire* and Lord Byron's epic *Childe Harold's Pilgrimage. The Consummation of Empire* shows a city very much like Rome at its height, while the scene of *Destruction* suggests an attack, such as the Vandal sack of Rome in 455.

The Course of Empire was donated to the New-York Historical Society in 1858.

The Consummation of Empire, 1836

Destruction, 1836

Desolation, 1836

THE SACK OF ROME (455)

In 455, the Vandal king Geiseric sailed his powerful fleet from the capital in Carthage, up the Tiber, finally sacking Rome. They plundered for two weeks, carrying away the treasures of the Temple of Peace and the gilded bronze tiles from the Temple of Jupiter. It was the second of three barbarian sacks of Rome.

Sack of Rome 455, by Karl Bryullov

PANTHEON, CAMPO DE' FIORI AND PIAZZA NAVONA

PONTE
UMBERTO I

VIA DI MONTE BRIANZO

LUNGOTEVERE MARZIO

VIA GIUSEPPE ZANARDELLI

VIA DELLA SCROFA

VIA DI
PALLACORDA

13

VIA DEI PREFETTI

VIA DELLA STELLETTA

VIA METASTASIO

VIA DEI PIANELLARI

Basilica di
Sant'Agostino
12

VIA DELLA COPPELLE

VIA IN AQUIRO

Santa Maria
della Pace

VIA DI SANTA MARIA DELL'ANIMA

Piazza
Navona

Fontana dei
Quattro Fiumi

9

Sant' Agnese
in Agone

8

San Luigi
dei Francesi
11

10

Palazzo
Madama

V. DEGLI STADERARI

VIA GIUSTINIANI

VIA DELLA DOGANA VECCHIA

The
Pantheon

1

VIA DEL SEMINARIO

VIA DELLA ROTONDA

VIA DEI CESTARI

Santa Maria
Sopra Minerva

2

VIA MONTERONE

VIA DI SANTA CHIARA

VIA DEL TEATRO VALLE

VIA DEL GOVERNO VECCHIO

VICOLO DELLA
CANCELLERIA

VIA LEUTANO

VIA DI PASQUINO

CORSO DEL RINASCIMENTO

7

CORSO VITTORIO EMANUELE II

VIA PAOLO SAVELLI

VIA DEL PELLEGRINO

DEI CAPPELLARI

6

VIA DEI BAULLARI

Piazza
Paradiso
3

CORSO VITTORIO EMANUELE II

VIA PARADISO

VIA DEL SUDARIO

VIA DI TORRE ARGENTINA

VIA DEL GESÙ

4

5

VIA DEL MONTE DELLA FARINA

VIA FLORIDA

A

VIA DI SANT'ANNA

San Carlo
ai Catinari

B

VIA DEGLI SPECCHI

Piazza
Bendetto
Cairoli

VIA ARENULA

VIA DEI FALEGNAMI

*Interior of the Pantheon,
Rome*, by Giovanni Paolo
Panini, c. 1734

From the Pantheon, the magnificent domed temple to all gods, to the Piazza Navona, a hub of public life since the Middle Ages, Rome's historic core, the *centro storico* sweeps in Republic-era ruins, Renaissance palazzo and one of the oldest marketplaces in Rome, the colorful, animated, Campo de' Fiori.

❧

1 "The Pantheon, so great within and without, has overwhelmed me with admiration," wrote Goethe after standing on the Piazza della Rotonda in November 1786. The bright square on which the Pantheon stands is named after the circular structure.

Fire destroyed the original Pantheon, which was built in 27 B.C. by Emperor Augustus's son-in-law, the noted engineer Marcus Agrippa. Emperor Hadrian started the decade-long rebuilding around 118 A.D., using fireproof pozzolan lime concrete instead of travertine limestone for its massive rounded walls and dome. The inscription attributing the work to Agrippa remains: M. AGRIPPA L. F. COS. TERTIUM FECIT. That is, Marcus Agrippia, son of Lucius, in his third council, made it.

The porch, with its sixteen massive classical columns and bronze doors leads to the cylindrical interior, often glowing gloriously thanks to an oculus, or circular window, in the dome. As Michelangelo said, the Pantheon seems as of "angelic and not human design."

Renaissance painter Raphael Sanzio and his bride-to-be Maria Bibbiena are among the luminaries buried here.

Take the Via della Rotonda to the right of the Pantheon entrance, and turn right into the first side street, Via della Palombella.

2 This will take you into the pretty little square, Piazza Sant'Eustachio, with its 9th-century Chiesa Sant'Eustachio dedicated to the Roman general Placidus, who was martyred around 100 A.D. after converting to Christianity. The church's cross is cradled within the antlers of a white stag, in keeping with a vision St. Eustachius had during a hunt.

The Caffè Sant'Eustachio is one of Rome's landmark coffee houses—a clamoring, aromatic

PANTHEON WITH BERNINI'S BELL TOWERS

Left: *The Pantheon and the Piazza della Rotonda,* by Rudolf Ritter von Alt, 1835; Right: *Pantheon of Agrippa,* 1880

den of coffee grinding and drinking, frequented by students, politicians, artists and tourists. With just a handful of tables out the front, most people have an espresso or cool *granita di caffè* standing *al bar*. Since 1999, brothers Raimondo and Roberto Ricci have put a strong ethical bent to the beans business, and organic or fair-trade sourced grinds sell along with a host of *tazze* (cups) and other souvenirs. The establishment's yellow logo features the Sant'Eustachio deer.

To the west of the café, is the start of the long, narrow Via del Teatro Valle.

Head south down this street until you encounter the square, Largo del Teatro Valle.

3 The small square faces south over the busy boulevard Corso Vittorio Emanuele II. Cross over this thoroughfare to the Piazza Vidoni, home to the Baroque 1591 church, Sant'Andrea della Valle—one of the settings in Puccini's opera *Tosca*.

On leaving the church, prepare to take a small but worthy detour. Turn right into the Corso Vittorio Emanuele II and head east about 500 feet to the Largo di Torre Argentina.

4 Turn right into the Via di Torre Argentina, which skirts the pit of archeological ruins called the Area Sacra di Largo Argentina (the Largo Argentina Sacred Area). Famed as a sanctuary for cats, the area was flattened between 1926 and 1929 in preparation for a luxury real estate development. In the process, several columns of four Republican-era temples, dating as far back as the 4th century B.C., first appeared.

The Death of Caesar (detail), by Vincenzo Camuccini, 1804-05

Although mostly covered by Via di Torre Argentina, the Curia Pompeii was once located behind the circular temple devoted to Aedes Fortunae Huiusce Diei (the "Luck of the Current Day"). This is where Julius Caesar was murdered on March 15, 44 B.C.

 Return to the Piazza Vidoni.

Head west on the Corso Vittorio Emanuele II and two streets along on your left is the lovely little Via Paradiso. Head down this street past the Piazza Paradiso, and into the Via del Biscione, which skirts the eastern side of the Campo de' Fiori. Turn right onto the piazza.

Bruno Giordano Monument

5 Framed by brightly colored houses, the Campo de' Fiori (field of flowers) retains the bustling and atmospheric flavor of the former medieval grain market. Open Monday through Saturday, the market is an authentic, local affair for flower, fruit and vegetable buyers and sellers, who gather here from 6 a.m. to early afternoon. In the Middle Ages, the area was used for high-profile executions, such as that of philosopher Bruno Giordano, whose statue stands in the center of the piazza in a hooded bronze cloak. Declared a heretic for his unorthodox views and meddling in Copernican (earth revolves around sun) astronomy, the heretic was burned on a huge pile of firewood in 1600.

Pallazo dellea Cancelleria, by Giuseppe Vasi, 18 century

6 Make your way back through the Campo de' Fiori to the Piazza della Cancelleria in the northern corner. The creamy façade of the Palazzo Cancelleria was built in the 15th century with blocks of travertine taken from the Colosseum. Its tenant, Cardinal Raffaele Riario, nephew of Pope Sixtus IV, was forced to leave the residence, after being caught participating in a plot to kill Pope Leo X in 1516.

A PALAZZO FARNESE AND B PALAZZO SPADA

One block south of the Campo de' Fiori, the Piazza Farnese is home to a High Renaissance palace, the Palazzo Farnese, which was re-designed by Michelangelo in 1534. Today it is the French Embassy and is not open to public. In Puccini's opera *Tosca*, it is the setting of the police headquarters in the second act.

One block to the east of the Palazzo Farnese is the Palazzo Spada, which was built in 1540 and acquired by Cardinal Spada in 1632. Borromini was commissioned to renovate the building, including the arched courtyard, which, by way of optical illusion, appears much longer than it is. The palace's Galleria Spada includes work by Artemisia and Orazio Gentileschi.

Left: *David Contemplating the Head of Goliath*, by Orazio Gentleschi, c. 1610; right: *St. Cecilia*, by Artemisia Gentileschi, c. 1616

7 Head northeast, and again over Corso Vittorio Emanuele, towards the Piazza di San Pantaleo. The 18th-century Palazzo Braschi is the seat of the Museo di Roma (Museum of Rome). Its collections of frescos, mosaics, ceramics, paintings, furniture, photographs and engravings from the Middle Ages to the mid-20th century are housed between here and Piazza Navona, 2.

Take the Via della Cuccagna, to the right of the museum entrance, to Piazza Navona.

Circo Agonalis

8 The distinctive oval-shaped piazza was once an ancient athletics stadium, built by Domitian around 90 A.D. The foot races or *agone* that took place here (and the stadium's name, Circo Agonalis) gave rise to the name Navona. The signs on the square still signal Piazza Navona–Stadio di Domiziano. The emperor abandoned his efforts to replace Rome's bloodthirsty gladiatorial contests with harmless

Greek-style games after one miserably attended season. The Baroque's famous architectural duo, Bernini and Borromini, transformed the 700-foot-long Stadium of Domitian into one of the exemplary public arenas of Italian daily life, with beautiful fountains, churches and palazzo.

9 Gian Lorenzo Bernini concocted the effervescent *Fontana dei Quattro Fiumi* (Fountain of the Four Rivers) while Francesco Borromini designed the white cupola-topped Chiesa di Sant'Agnese in Agone, built on the spot where St. Agnes was martyred. Borromini incorporated part of the façade of the neighboring Palazzo Pamphilj into his church; the Pamphilj doves nesting on the entry columns are part of the heraldry of the family of Pope Innocent X, Giovanni Battista Pamphilj.

If you are not yet tired, you may wish to continue on a Caravaggio tour, starting from the Piazza Navona.

10 Walk towards the opposite side of Sant'Agnese (east) and leave Piazza Navona to Corso del Rinasciment, where. Palazzo Madama, home to Italian Senate, stands. Caravaggio once lived here when the palazzo was home of his patron, Cardinal Del Monte.

11 Heading north, turn right on Via del Salvatore. At the first corner on your left is San Luigi dei Francesi, home to three of Caravaggio's most famous paintings. Walk towards the back of the church where you will find the Contarelli Chapel. *The Calling of Saint Matthew*, *The Martyrdom of Saint Matthew* (1599-1600) and *The Inspiration of Saint Matthew* (1602), are still in the chapel for which they were commissioned, winning Caravaggio his first major public fame at 27 years

The Prophet Isaiah

12 Walk north on Via della Scrofa, one of Caravaggio's regular haunts, and turn left at Villa del Coppelle to Piazza Sant'Agostino. Behind the exterior of the basicilia are Caravaggio's painting *Madonna di Loreto* and *Raphael*'s fresco *The Prophet Isaiah*.

13 Return to Via della Scrofa and walk two blocks further north. Turn right into Via dei Prefetti, then immediately left, into Via di Pallacorda, where Caravaggio killed Ranuccio Tomassoni in a hot-blooded feud after a tennis game. Caravaggio fled Rome, and died before he could return. The detailed story of the incident is on the plaque at the entrance to the Adriana Hotel.

Go back to the Via della Scrofa and return to Piazza Navona.

Then & Now

Left: *View of the Piazza Navona on the ruins of the Circus Agonale*, by G.B. Piranesi, 1756

CARAVAGGIO IN ROME'S CHURCHES

■ San Luigi dei Francesi

■ Sant'Agostino

■ Santa Maria del Popolo

1. *The Calling of Saint Matthew*, 1599-1600 **2.** *The Martyrdom of Saint Matthew*, 1599-1600 **3.** *The Inspiration of Saint Matthew*, 1602, San Luigi dei Francesi **4.** *Madonna di Loreto*, c.1604-06, Sant'Agostino **5.***Crucifixion of St. Peter*, 1600 **6.** *Conversion on the Way to Damascus*, 1601, Santa Maria del Popolo

SANT'ANGELO, SAN PIETRO / ST. PETER'S AND VATICAN MUSEUMS

1 Ponte Sant'Angelo
2 Castel Sant'Angelo
3 St. Peter's Square
4 Vatican Obelisk
5 St. Peter's Basilica
6 Vatican Museums

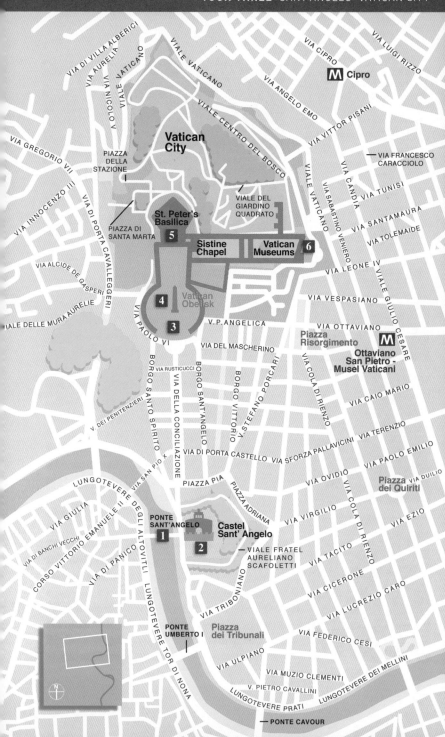

VIA DI VILLA ALBERICI

VIA AURELIA

VIALE VATICANO

VIA CIPRO

VIA LUIGI RIZZO

Ⓜ Cipro

VIA NICOLO V

VIALE VATICANO

VIA ANGELO EMO

VIA VITTOR PISANI

VIA GREGORIO VII

VIALE CENTRO DEL BOSCO

VIA FRANCESCO CARACCIOLO

VIA INNOCENZO III

PIAZZA DELLA STAZIONE

Vatican City

VIALE VATICANO

VIA CANDIA

VIA TUNISI

VIA DI PORTA CAVALLEGGERI

VIALE DEL GIARDINO QUADRATO

VIA SANTAMAURA

VIA SABASTIAO VENIERO

VIA TOLEMAIDE

VIA ALCIDE DE GASPERI

PIAZZA DI SANTA MARTA

St. Peter's Basilica

5

Sistine Chapel

Vatican Museums

6

VIA LEONE IV

VIALE DELLE MURA AURELIE

VIA PAOLO VI

4

Vatican Obelisk

VIA VESPASIANO

VIALE GIULIO CESARE

3

V. P. ANGELICA

VIA OTTAVIANO

VIA DEI PENITENZIERI

BORGO SANTO SPIRITO

VIA RUSTICUCCI

BORGO SANT'ANGELO

VIA DEL MASCHERINO

Piazza Risorgimento

Ottaviano San Pietro - Musei Vaticani

Ⓜ

VIA CAIO MARIO

VIA DELLA CONCILIAZIONE

BORGO VITTORIO

V. STEFANO PORCARI

VIA COLA DI RIENZO

VIA TERENZIO

VIA DI PORTA CASTELLO

VIA SFORZA PALLAVICINI

VIA PAOLO EMILIO

VIA SAN PIO X

PIAZZA PIA

PIAZZA ADRIANA

VIA OVIDIO

VIA VIRGILIO

VIA COLA DI RIENZO

Piazza dei Quiriti

VIA DUILIO

VIA EZIO

LUNGOTEVERE DEGLI ALTOVITI

1

PONTE SANT'ANGELO

Castel Sant' Angelo

2

VIA TACITO

VIA GIULIA

VIA DI BANCHI VECCHI

CORSO VITTORIO EMANUELE II

VIA DI PANICO

VIALE FRATEL AURELIANO SCAFOLETTI

VIA CICERONE

VIA LUCREZIO CARO

LUNGOTEVERE TOR DI NONA

PONTE UMBERTO I

Piazza dei Tribunali

VIA TRIBONIANO

VIA FEDERICO CESI

VIA ULPIANO

VIA MUZIO CLEMENTI

V. PIETRO CAVALLINI

LUNGOTEVERE DEI MELLINI

LUNGOTEVERE PRATI

PONTE CAVOUR

START:
Ponte Sant'Angelo :
Bus No. 40 to Lungotevere
Vaticano or Metro, Linea A,
Lepanto

END:
Vatican Museums : Metro,
Linea A, Ottaviano or
Cipro. Bus No. 49

Tour Time:
About 4 hours

Chapters:
6, 13, 15, 16, 17, 19, 23, 27

Michelangelo's *Pietà* at St. Peter's Basilica

After Rome's founding, the marshy area on
the right side of the Tiber was called the
Ager Vaticanus, Vatican Field, possibly after
a vanished Etruscan settlement, Vaticum. The
hive of gloriously decorated religious edifices
which graces it today sprung up from a grim
history of religious persecution, with Emperor
Nero's wholesale martyrdom of Christians in
64 A.D. taking place at his arena on the Mons
Vaticanus hill. Since the Middle Ages, the
history of the Tiber riverbank's stronghold, the
Castel Sant'Angelo, has been entwined with
that of the Basilica dedicated to St. Peter.

1 For nearly 2,000 years the Ponte Sant'Angelo
bridge has connected the city to the Castel
Sant'Angelo and western bank of the Tiber. Built by
Hadrian in 134 A.D. and originally called the Pons
Aelius, it was the main pilgrim way for worshippers
heading to St. Peter's until the late 15th century. A
drowning disaster during the Jubilee of 1450 led to
a revamp of the bridge.

In 1667, Gian Lorenzo Bernini sculpted his glorious cloud-floating angels for the bridge, on the request of Pope Clement IX. The angels seem to float through the air swooning, their wings and faces transformed by the sculpting master of movement.

2 Towering over the Tiber-side, the Castel Sant'Angelo surges atop the vaulted tomb of Emperor Hadrian, which was converted to a military fortress at the turn of the 5th century. Swept within the Aurelian Walls, the stronghold got its name in the 6th-century from Pope Gregory the Great, who dreamt of archangel Michael sheathing his sword after a terrible plague. Through the Middle Ages, patrician families who controlled the papacy claimed it as their personal fortress. The underground *passetto*—built around 1280 by the Orsini pope, Nicholas III, to link the bastion to the Vatican—was used as an escape route for Pope Clement VII during the sack of Rome in May 1527. In 1367, Pope Urban V got hold of the keys to the castle, from then on used as a court, lock-up and execution chamber for political prisoners, as well as papal hideout, and home to the Vatican treasury and library.

Bridge of Aelius and Hadrian's Mausoleum, by Johann Bernhard Fischer Von Erlach (1656-1723)

The bastion was converted to a prison and barracks in the 1600s. In the finale of Puccini's *Tosca*, the heroine leaps from the rooftop to her death after the shooting of her lover; actual executions were made in the small interior square.

Pope Gregory I (detail), by Francisco de Zurbarán, 1626-27

The entry to the castle lies on the Lungotevere Castello—the thoroughfare skirting the Tiber changes its name along its course according to geography, from the Lungotevere Castello to Lungotevere Vaticano and to the Lungotevere Gianicolense, under the Gianicolo Hill.

Mausoleum of Hadrian, now called the Castel S. Angelo, by G. B. Piranesi, c. 1756

A visit to the castle includes Hadrian's mausoleum and the ramparts; the lavishly decorated papal quarters, spread across six levels from the basement through various bastions; and the rooftop *terrazza* dell'Angelo with its angel statue.

Leaving the castle, head west through the Piazza Giovanni XXIII.

After crossing the hectic Viale Fratel Porfirio Ciprari, you will find yourself at the beginning of the Via della Conciliazione, which leads to Piazza San Pietro.

3 Bernini's St. Peter's Square is actually a monumental oval, 787 feet wide and connected to the basilica's façade by a distinct trapezoidal or lozenge-shaped quadrangle. As the mother of all churches, said Bernini, its entrance had to make a statement—welcoming Catholics with open arms, while uniting and enlightening heretics.

The vast elliptical piazza is clutched by two outstretched arms of statue-tipped colonnades, double rows of columns curved around its southern

Then & Now

Left: *Old Staint Peter's*, by H.W. Brewer, c. late 19th century, illustrates how St. Peter's Basilica likely appeared around 1450. The Vatican Obelisk is shown on the left.

and northern sides. In all, there are 372 columns (284 Doric columns and 88 pilasters of travertine marble) topped by statues. A team of Bernini's pupils sculpted the 140 saint statues over four decades, starting in 1661.

4 The Vatican Obelisk was unveiled on the square in September 1586, after a dramatic effort to relocate it the short distance from Vatican Hill. The 85-foot red granite monolith, the second tallest of Rome's ancient obelisks, was brought to the city by Caligula in 37 A.D.

The obelisk is straddled by fountains: the one on the right facing the basilica is the work of Carlo Maderno in 1614; that on the left was added by Bernini in 1675, for symmetry's sake.

5 During Nero's crucifixion spectacles, tradition holds that St. Peter was crucified head down. Following Emperor Constantine's Edict of Milan of 313 A.D., which swept in religious tolerance, he honored St. Peter with a church to house his tomb. Consecrated in 329, the crumbling basilica was on its last legs by the 14th century. During the Renaissance beautification of Rome, Pope Julius II assigned architect Donato Bramante the job of redesigning the Basilica di San Pietro, St. Peter's Basilica, in 1505. During the 150-year construction process, the church was blessed by some of history's greatest creative talents: Raphael Sanzio shaped the 623-foot long basilica into a Latin cross in 1514; Michelangelo added the *Pietà* statue, then the 1588 dome, completed after his death by Domenico Fontana; Carlo Maderno created the Corinthian columned façade in 1614; and Bernini brought the gorgeous post-finishing touches of the square and the baldachin.

On the northern side of St. Peter's Square, pass through Bernini's arcade of columns, the Largo del Colonatto, and take the Via di Porta Antica ("the way of the ancient gateway to Rome), into the Via di Porta Angelica.

Continue north, along the Via di Porta Angelica, until it meets Piazza del Risorgimento and turn left.

Heading west, trace the Vatican walls along Viale Vaticano, following the signs to the Musei Vaticani.

The Viale Vaticano swerves left around the Vatican Palace walls. Stick with them, climbing southwards to join the queues to the Vatican Museums, which can be avoided by booking online.

6 With treasures scattered over five miles of corridors, one could easily spend a day or two at the Vatican Museums. Allow at least three hours to see some of the highlights: the Sistine Chapel, Raphael's Rooms, the Pinacoteca, the Borgia Apartments, and the Egyptian, Etruscan and Ethnological Museums. Do not miss special exhibitions, which range from the spirituality of Aboriginal Australians to Fabergé's sacred icons for Russian Czars. Starting with a collection of Pope Julius II's sculptures, in 1503, the Museums gradually incorporated individual papal collections, archaeology and classical antiquity through the 18th and 19th centuries.

In 1508, Raphael began to fresco the Vatican apartments (the Stanze di Raffaello) as Michelangelo started on the ceiling of the Sistine

The courtyard of the Vatican Museums

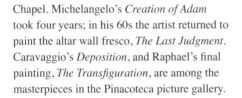

Chapel. Michelangelo's *Creation of Adam* took four years; in his 60s the artist returned to paint the altar wall fresco, *The Last Judgment*. Caravaggio's *Deposition*, and Raphael's final painting, *The Transfiguration*, are among the masterpieces in the Pinacoteca picture gallery.

The Vatican Museums are open Monday–Saturday. Ticket office is open 9:00 a.m.–4:00 p.m. Museums close at 6:00 p.m. Various guided tours take in the museums and Sistine Chapel, the Vatican gardens and St. Peter's Basilica, while themed visits include art and faith or art and music.

THE BORGIA APARTMENT

When Alexander VI was elected Pope in 1492, the fourteen rooms of the Vatican's private chambers were frescoed by early Renaissance master Pinturicchio, who worked on the project for two years. The Borgia Apartment is located between Raphael's rooms and the Sistine Chapel in the Vatican Museum Tour.

1 Sala delle Sibille
In 1500, Alfonso of Aragon, the second husband of Lucrezia Borgia was assassinated in this room. Cesare Borgia was imprisoned here after he was arrested in Ostia in 1502 by Julius II.

4 Sala delle Arti Liberali
Alexander VI's study. After his death by malaria in 1503 his body was placed here; his skin turned black from the heat.

5 Sala dei Santi
The famous fresco, *St. Catherine's Disputation*, was modeled on the likeness of Lucrezia Borgia. *The Virgin and Child With Angels* is located right above the entrance of the next room. The models for the Virgin and Child were Julia Farnese and her infant Laura, daughter of Alexander VI.

6 Sala dei Mister
The fresco, *Resurrection*, shows Alexander VI and his four sons.

13 Alexander VI's Bedroom
Site of the Borgia pope's last breath.

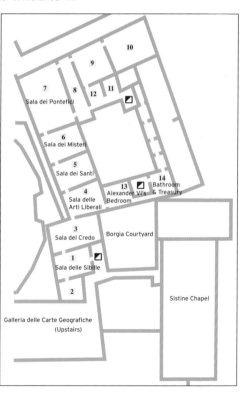

HIGHLIGHTS FROM THE VATICAN MUSEUMS

1. *San Girolamo*, by Leonardo da Vinci, c. 1480 **2.** *The School of Athens*, by Raphael, 1510–11
3. *The Last Judgment*, by Michelangelo, 1537–41 **4.** *Sarcophagus of St. Helena*, c. 4th century
5. *Laocoön and His Sons*, 25 B.C. **6.** *Transfiguration*, by Raphael, 1518–20 **7.** *Apollo Belvedere*,
c. 120–140; copy of bronze original of ca. 350–325 B.C. **8.** *The Entombment of Christ*, by
Caravaggio, 1602–03

TRASTEVERE

1 Piazza Mastai
2 Basilica di Santa Maria in Trastevere
3 Museo di Roma in Trastevere
4 San Pietro in Montorio
5 Independence War Memorial
6 Fontana dell'Acqua Paola

7 Romolo nel Giardino della Fornarina
8 Porta Settimiana
9 Villa Farnesina
10 Palazzo Corsini
11 Orto Botanico
A Santa Cecilia in Trastevere

10

9

Villa Farnesina

11 VIA CORSINO

V.D PARCO DI VILLA CORSINI

LUNGOTEVERE DELLA FARNESIN

Trastevere

VIA DI PORTA SAN PANCRAZIO

VIA GARIBALDI

VICOLO DEL LEOPARDO

VIA DEL MATTONATO

VIA DELLA LUNGARA

8

7

6

VIA GIACOMO MEDICI

VIA GARIBALDI

VIA DEI PANIERI

VICOLO DEL BOLOGNA

LUNGOTEVERE DEI TEBALDI

5

4

San Pietro in Montorio

VICOLO DELLA FRUSTA

VICOLO DEL CEDRO

3

VICOLO DE' CINQUE

VIA DELLA PELLICCIA

PONTE SISTO

VIA GARIBALDI

VIA GOFFREDO MAMELI

VIA DELLA PAGLIA

VIA DEL MORO

VIA DELLA LUNGARA

VIA LUIGI MASI

Santa Maria in Trastevere

2

VIA DELLA RENELLA

VIA DELLA POLITEAMA

VIA GIACOMO VENEZIAN

VIA AGNOSTINO BERTANI

VIA LUCIANO MANARA

VIA DI SAN COSIMATO

VIA DELLA CISTERNA

PONTI GARIBALDI

VIA ROMA LIBERIA

VIA DI SAN FRANCESCO A RIPE

VIA DEI FIENAROLI

VIA EMILIO MOROSINI

VIA NATALE DEL GRANDE

VIA DI SAN GALLICANO

LUNGOTEVERE RAFFAELLO SANZIO

VIA DELLE FRATTE DI TRASTEVERE

PIAZZA SIDNEY SONNINO

VIALE DI TRASTEVERE

1

Piazza Mastai

VIA DEI GENOVESI

Confraternita Di S. Giovanni Battista Dei Genovesi

VIA DELLA LUCE

San Francesco a Ripa

VIA ANICIA

A

Santa Cecilia in Trastevere

START:
Piazza Mastai: Tram Line H

END:
Villa Farnesina: Walk 850
meters on the Via della
Lungara, to the bus stop
Chiesa Nuova and take
Bus 40

Tour Time:
About 4 hours

Chapters:
11, 18, 19, 24

Medieval Houses at Santa Cecilia, Trastevere, by Roesler
Franz, c. 1880

The district across the river Tiber, as
Trastevere's name literally translates, is a
world apart. Settled by Etruscans, it shot up
in the Middle Ages as a thriving, cosmopolitan
quarter for merchants, artisans, Christians and
Jews. Backing into the Gianicolo, or Janiculum
Hill, its hive of medieval streets and pretty
piazzas is dabbed with fountains and churches.

1 This car-free, cobbled piazza of Piazza Mastai
lies alongside the Trastevere's main thoroughfare,
the Viale di Trastevere. Heavily frequented by
locals on hot evenings, its late Renaissance turtle
fountain, Fontana delle Tartarughe, is decorated
with symbols of Pope Pio (Pius) IX.

Cross the Viale di Trastevere, turn left into the Via
delle Fratte di Trastevere, then right into Via di San
Francesco a Ripa—the street and the church are
named after Rome's big river port, the Ripa Grande,
which was abandoned in the 19th century.

Continue along, until your reach the small Piazza San Calisto.

2 Turn right into Via di San Cosimato to reach San Calisto's famous neighbor, Piazza Santa Maria in Trastevere.

The Piazza is the Trastevere's most animated hub for young and old, a colorful crossroads of newspaper vendors, café crowds, children on bicycles and churchgoers. Its central fountain is a favorite vantage point for admiring the adjacent church, or pausing to eat a gelato.

The exquisite 12th-century Basilica di Santa Maria in Trastevere looms over the square, with its gilded Baroque interiors, Romanesque *campanile* and splendid mosaics. Built on the foundations of a much older church, its shimmering mosaic apse was decorated in the Baroque period.

Turn left into Via della Lungaretta, which swerves around the side of the church and merges into the Via della Paglia.

A SANTA CECILIA IN TRASTEVERE

Near Piazza Mastai, Santa Cecilia in Trastevere was built over the home of St. Cecilia, a woman of noble descent who owned a house on this site in the 3rd century. The present church was built by Pope Paschal I, who reigned from 817-24.

Cecilia and her husband, Valerian, were martyred because of their Christian convictions. After a failed attempt to burn Cecilia alive in a scalding hot bath, the executor tried to behead her with an axe. She died of her wounds three days later, while continuing to hand out alms to the poor.

In 1599, her body was found, incorrupt and complete with deep axe cuts in her neck. This miraculous event caught the attention of Pope Clement VIII who immediately commissioned Stefano Maderno to sculpt the martyred saint. The naturalistic sculpture is Maderno's masterpiece.

Church and Monastery of St. Egidio in Trastevere, by Giuseppe Vasi (1710-1782)

Tempietto di San Pietro in Montorio

3 Turn right into the Piazza di Sant'Egidio on which you will find the Museo di Roma in Trastevere, with its various permanent and temporary collections, covering topics from the story of Columbus and other explorers to 18th- and 19th-century paintings, prints and drawings.

Exit and turn left into the Vicolo dell Cedro.

Continue along this curvaceous laneway, which leads to a very steep but short staircase up to the main road, Via Garibaldi.

Cross over carefully, as there is a sharp bend in this forested road.

Almost directly opposite, a stone walkway cuts through the foothills of the Gianicolo. Initially marked Passagio Pubblico (public passageway), as it winds around the hill, you will see its name as the Via di S.Pietro in Montorio.

The passage leads to the Piazza di San Pietro in Montorio or "mountain of gold." The hilltop square offers one of the best panoramas in Rome—in the afternoon, the setting sun projects onto the Eternal City.

4 The Piazza di San Pietro in Montorio is named after the 15th-century church San Pietro in Montorio, a treasure chest of art with a chapel by Gian Lorenzo Bernini called the Capella Raimondi and a wonderful view from its terrazzo. In the cloister to the right of the main chapel lies the main attraction: the Tempietto di San Pietro in Montorio. The "little temple" is said to mark the spot where St. Peter's cross once stood. Donato Bramante, the chief architect of the redesigned St.Peter's Basilica

The Crucifixion of St. Peter (detail), by Michelangelo, c. 1546-50, the Cappella Paolina, Vatican City

designed this Neoclassical shrine, with its miniature cupola and granite columns and balustrades, in 1502. The adjacent Real Academia di Espana, organizes visits to the Tempietto, and holds art and cultural exhibitions.

Walk behind the church, to the left of the entry, and cross Via Garibaldi.

5 A bit further along is a war memorial dedicated to those who died in the Italian independence wars between 1848 and 1870. In 1849, the Janiculum Hill was the scene of a battle between French troops, fighting on behalf of the pope, and Guiseppe Garibaldi's troops, defending the Roman Republic. The monument is marked with the words "*Roma o morte*"—Rome or death—the famous phrase pronounced by Garibaldi.

6 One hundred feet up the road is a milk-white fountain, the Fontana dell'Acqua Paola, known by Romans as "il fontanone" (the big fountain). It is not only the fountain but the views which brim over here, though the vistas from the Belvedere Niccolò Scatoli are somewhat impeded by the rooftops in front.

241

Return to the church, down the Via di S.Pietro in Montorio until you again encounter the Via Garibaldi.

Turn left and descend to the base of the street, at the intersection of Via della Scala. (Note, if you want to cut short the walking, take the Navette Gianicolo/ bus 115 down Via Garibaldi and get off rested for the following leg of the walk).

7 At left far corner of the intersection of Via Garibaldi and Via della Scala, is Romolo nel Giardino della Fornarina, a restaurant located in a 16th-century house. Margherita Luti, the famous "Fornarina" and mistress of Raphael, lived here, and it was here she posed for him.

8 Turn left and pass through the crenulated 3rd-century doorway, the Porta Settimiana. Named after 2nd-century Emperor Septimius Severus, and possibly used as an access to his public baths, it subsequently served as an opening in the fortified Aurelian Wall.

The door leads into the Via della Lungara. Several streets in Trastevere are named after their lingering eternity and Lungara (from the word for long) is the finest example. Follow the signs pointing to "Villa Farnesina, Raffaelo's frescoes."

9 On the right, at Via della Lungara 230, is Villa Farnesina, built in 1511 as a pleasure palace for Agostino Chigi, treasurer to Pope Julius II and major patron of Raphael, whose frescoes adorn the various *loggias*. (Open 9 a.m.–1 p.m. Mon–Sat)

10 Opposite, at Via della Lungara, 10, is the 16th-century Palazzo Corsini, which houses part of the collection of the Galleria Nazionale d'Arte Antica. The Galleria Corsini showcases paintings by Murillo and Rubens, as well as the apartment of Swedish Queen Christina, who after abdicating and converting to Catholicism in the mid-1600s, spent the rest of her life in Rome, at this address.

11 If you wish to extend your walk and drench yourself in fresh-aired greenery, head to the botanical gardens. Leave the museum, retrace your steps up the Via della Lungara to Via Corsini, and turn right. The small street leads to the entry of the Orto Botanico, which are like a footnote on the Gianicolo Hill.

RAPHAEL AND LA FORNARINA IN TRASTEVERE

Raphael was so smitten with the *Fornarina* that he was unable to finish his work for Agostino Chigi at his Villa Farnesina. The temptation to escape to Via della Lungara and his lovely *Fornarina* was just too strong. Chigi purportedly found a practical solution, bringing Margherita Luti to live in his palazzo until Raphael completed his project.

Their love story ended with Raphael's premature death in 1520—some chroniclers attributed the deadly fever he suffered to a night of excessive sex with Luti. Four months after the artist's death, the Trastevere convent of Sant'Apollonia registered the arrival of "widow Margherita", daughter of a Siena baker.

PIAZZA BARBERINI, QUIRINALE HILL AND FONTANA DI TREVI

1 Santa Maria della Vittoria
2 Fountain of Triton
3 Palazzo Barberini
4 Palazzo del Quirinale

5 Piazza del Quirinale
6 Scuderie del Quirinale
7 Trevi Fountain
A Galleria Colonna

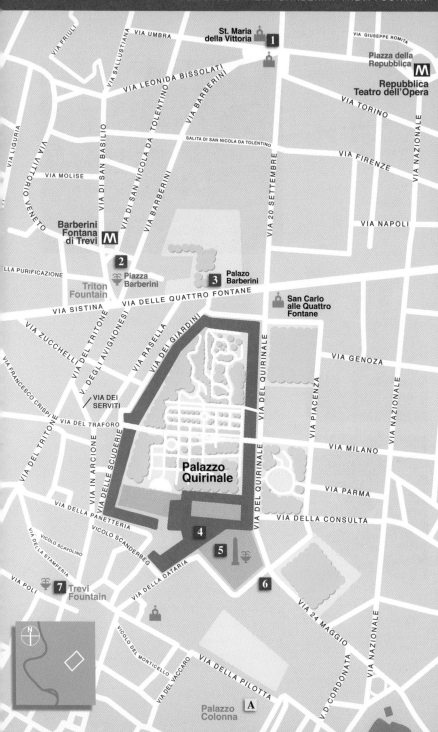

START:
The Piazza della
Ripubblica: Metro Linea A

END:
Trevi Fountain : Bus 492
or from nearby Via del
Tritone Bus 175

Tour Time:
About 3 hours

Chapters:
19, 23, 29, 30

As you travel from Santa Maria della Vittoria through to the Piazza di Trevi, the architecture and sculpture of 17th-century Baroque star Gian Lorenzo Bernini will accompany you; his fountains, his palazzo façades, his animated and pious marble marvels, and other works inspired by his originality. A vast number of his creations would not have seen the light of day if it had not been for the patronage of Pope Urban VIII, Maffeo Barberini, whose name is equally engraved into Baroque Rome. Architect Francesco Borromini rounds off the Baroque's trail-blazing trio who, with the help of hundreds of other designers and artists, transformed the city.

1 Take Via Orlando northwest from Piazza della Repubblica to Via XX Settembre. At the intersection of Santa Maria della Vittoria stands as a Roman Catholic basilica dedicated to the Virgin Mary, built in 1605. The church is known for the masterpiece of Gian Lorenzo Bernini in the Cornaro Chapel, the *Ecstasy of Saint Teresa*, which stirred up Rome and confirmed Bernini's status as the city's marble maestro.

Walk westwards on Via Barberini to Piazza Barberini.

2 One of several piazza centerpieces by Bernini— his Fontana del Tritone (Triton Fountain) in Piazza Barberini features Poseidon's son, Triton, trumpeting water through a conch shell. The half man half fish is perched high on a crimped scallop shell, carried by four dolphins. Made for Bernini's major papal patron, Urban VIII, the fountain sports the Barberini family coat of arms. In the piazza's northern corner, near Via Veneto, the minute Fontana delle Api (the "Bee Fountain"), another Bernini work, is a tribute to the Barberini family's apian symbol.

Piazza Barberini, by Ettore Roesler Franz, c.1880

Exit the southern end of the piazza, turn left onto the Via delle Quattro Fontane.

3 At Via delle Quattro Fontane, 13, is the National Gallery of Ancient Art (Galleria Nazionale d'Arte Antica), at the Palazzo Barberini. Cardinal Matteo Barberini's home was completed by Bernini and Borromini a decade after he became Pope Urban VIII in 1623. Set within lush gardens, the palazzo's façade was made from breakaway bits of travertine from the Colosseum. The gallery is a treasure chest of Medieval and Renaissance art with a major focus on Raphael, Florentine and Venetian painters. Its crowning glory is a fresco by Pietro da Cortona, which shares the limelight with Raphael's *La Fornarina*. (Open Tues–Sun, 8 a.m.–7 p.m., Closed Dec 25, Jan 1).

PALAZZO BARBERINI

The helicoidal staircase by Borromini

The Palazzo Barberini in Via delle Quattro Fontane, is home to part of the treasures of the Galleria Nazionale d'arte antica, the National Gallery of Ancient Art. Rivals Borromini and Bernini worked on finishing this glorious building for Matteo Barberini, a decade after he became Pope Urban VIII in 1623.

Its lofty centerpiece is Pietro da Cortona's fresco in the main hall, the *Trionfo della Divina Provvidenza*. The oceanic mural shows Providence wrapped in a golden mantle and seated on clouds, her head in a halo of light. Around her are various figures—Purity, Justice, Mercy, Truth and Beauty—while the naked, feather-winged Cronus has a field day devouring his children, thus eliminating terrible time. The Barberini family bathes in the eternal glory and benediction of Immortality, who flutters above their coat of arms in a crown of stars.

The Barberini collection includes paintings from the Middle Ages to the 18th century. Highlights include Caravaggio's *Judith Beheading Holofernes*, 1598-99, and Titian's *Venus and Adonis*, painted in 1560.

1. *La Fornarina (Portrait of a young woman)*, by Raphael, 1518-19 **2.** *Narciso*, by Caravaggio, 1597-99 **3.** *Judith Beheading Holofernes*, by Caravaggio, 1598-99 **4.** *Allegory of Divine Providence* (detail), by Pietro da Cortona, c.1633-39

Cross over Via delle Quattro Fontane, in front of
the gallery, turn right and take the first street on
your left, the Via Rassela. This street has a haunting
past: In 1944, a communist partisan group carried
out a bomb attack here, killing 33 German officers;
in retaliation, 10 Italian civilians were sentenced to
death for each German soldier killed.

Descend Via Rassela about 400 feet until you come
to Via del Traforo; cross over and continue directly
on onto Via in Arcione, until the intersection with
Via del Paneterria. Again cross over, into Via del
Lavatore and take the first turn to the left, the
narrow Vicolo Scanderbeg.

At the end of this sinewy passageway, turn left onto
Via della Dataria and up the wide staircase, Salita di
Montecavallo—with statues tucked in niches in its
walls—to the Piazza del Quirinale.

4 The Palazzo del Quirinale was envisioned in
1574 by Gregory XIII as a summer residence for
the popes, up in the fresher air of the Quirinal
Hill. Architect Flaminio Ponzio's building was
completed on his death by Carlo Maderno.

Then & Now

Left: *Piazza del Quirinale*, by G. B. Piranesi, 1773

Scuderie del Quirinale, by
Giuseppe Vasi, 1739

5 The Quirinal Hill became known as Monte Cavallo, after being graced in 1589 with its colossal statues of horses—*cavalli*. The square's showpiece fountain, Fontana dei Dioscuri (the "Horse-Tamers of Monte Cavallo") is based on the legend of Castor and Pollux, the brothers of Helen of Troy. Domenico Fontana's fountain was part of the piazza's makeover by Renaissance wonder-builder Pope Sixtus V. Nearly two centuries later, Pope Pius VI shifted the Quirinal Obelisk from Augustus's mausoleum to place between the bare-bottomed strongmen.

6 Opposite, on the corner of Via XXIV Maggio and Via Dataria, is the Scuderie del Quirinale, the former palace stables turned into a store of fine art. The gallery is open only during temporary—though generally knockout—exhibitions, on artists such as Sandro Botticelli and Tintoretto.

Retrace your journey down the stairway into Via della Dataria, then all the way to the end, and turn right into Via di San Vincenzo. Turn left into the Piazza di Trevi; the Via del Lavatore will be on your right.

7 The Trevi Fountain is one of Rome's most iconic landmarks, its name coming from the three roads, "*tre vie*" that converge on the piazza. Though virtually impossible to separate from the iconic Anita Ekberg scene in Fellini's 1960s classic, *La Dolce Vita*, the history of the Fontana di Trevi goes back two centuries earlier. The foaming Baroque daydream of sea gods and sea beasts was completed in 1762, three decades after architect Nicola Salvi won the competition to design a new fountain for Clement XII.

Salvi picked up on a design by Bernini, which had been ditched several decades earlier. Salvi was a follower of Bernini—as were many of the team of nine sculptors who worked on the project—as the effusive gushing fountain of horn-blowing Tritons, travertine, oyster shell chariots and sea horses testifies; all are Berninian motifs.

The 66-foot-wide font's insatiable thirst is fed by the ancient Roman aqueduct, the Aqua Virgo.

Toss a coin in the fountain to guarantee your return to the city.

A SATURDAY TOUR OF THE GALLERIA COLONNA

After viewing Rome's famous palaces, step inside the Palazzo Colonna, one of the city's oldest and largest private residences. Since the Middle Ages some twenty generations of the powerful Colonna family have lived here. The palazzo's Galleria Colonna is open to public every Saturday from 9 a.m. to 1:15 p.m. Inside, you can see masterpieces from the family's private collection including works by Lorenzo Monaco, Domenico Ghirlandaio, Palma the Elder, Salviati, Bronzino, Tintoretto, Pietro da Cortona, Annibale Carracci, Guercino, Francesco Albani, Muziano and Guido Reni.

In the final scene of the 1950s cinema classic, *Roman Holiday*, Audrey Hepburn, playing Princess Anne, held a press conference in the palazzo's spectacular Sala Grande.

From the Piazza del Quirinale retrace your journey down the stairway into Via della Dataria, then all the way to the end, and turn left into Via della Pillotta. The entrance of the Galleria Colonna is located at Via della Pillotta, 17.

Top: Sala Grande; left: *The Beaneater*, by Annibale Carracci, 1580-90, Galleria Colonna

PIAZZA DI SPAGNA, PINCIO HILL AND PIAZZA DEL POPOLO

1 Piazza di Spagna
2 Keats-Shelley House
3 Chiesa della Trinità dei Monti
4 Villa Medici
5 Collis Hortulorum
6 Piazza Bucaresti
7 Basilica di Santa Maria del Popolo
8 Porta del Popolo

9 Chiesa di Santa Maria de Montesanto and Chiesa di Santa Maria dei Miracoli
10 Canova and Rosati
11 Casa di Goethe
12 Via della Croce
13 Antico Caffè Greco

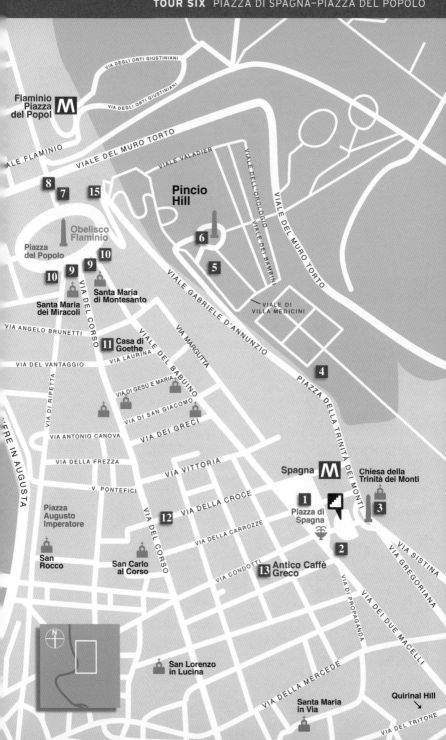

VIA DEGLI ORTI GIUSTINIANI

VIA DEGLI ORTI GIUSTINIANI

Flaminio
Piazza
del Popol M

ALE FLAMINIO

VIALE DEL MURO TORTO

VIALE VALADIER

8 7 15

Pincio
Hill

Obelisco
Flaminio

6

Piazza
del Popolo

5

10
10 9 9

Santa Maria
di Montesanto

Santa Maria
dei Miracoli

VIA ANGELO BRUNETTI

11 Casa di
Goethe

VIA DEL VANTAGGIO

VIA LAURINA

VIA DI RIPETTA

VIA DI GESÙ E MARIA

VIA DI SAN GIACOMO

VIA ANTONIO CANOVA

VIA DEI GRECI

VIA DELLA FREZZA

V. PONTEFICI

Piazza
Augusto
Imperatore

San
Rocco

San Carlo
al Corso

12

VIA DEL CORSO

VIA VITTORIA

VIA DELLA CROCE

VIA DELLA CARROZZE

VIA CONDOTTI

13 Antico Caffè
Greco

VIALE DEL MURO TORTO

VIALE DELL'OROLOGIO

VIALE DEI BAMBINI

VIALE DI
VILLA MEDICINI

VIALE GABRIELE D'ANNUNZIO

VIA MARGUTTA

VIALE DEL BABUINO

4

PIAZZA DELLA TRINITÀ DEI MONTI

Spagna M

Chiesa della
Trinità dei Monti

1

Piazza di
Spagna

2

3

VIA SISTINA

VIA GREGORIANA

VIA DI PROPAGANDA

VIA DEI DUE MACELLI

ERE IN AUGUSTA

N

San Lorenzo
in Lucina

VIA DELLA MERCEDE

Santa Maria
in Via

Quirinal Hill
→

VIA DEL TRITONE

START:
Piazza di Spagna:
Metro Line A

END:
Piazza di Spagna:
Metro Line A

Tour Time:
About 4 hours

Chapters:
9, 20, 21, 23, 24, 25, 26

Piazza di Spagna

The zone between the Piazza di Spagna and the Pincio Hill is among the most atmospheric in Rome. Dense in history, religion, culture and nature, it has been a favorite haunt for writers, poets, artists and musicians since the 18th century. From the hillside, the Trinita dei Monti church sanctifies its surrounds, while the Pincio gardens steep the neighborhood in cool, cultured greenery and ancient horticultural tradition.

1 The Piazza di Spagna and Spanish Steps were created by architect Francesco de Sanctis in the early 18th century and named after the Spanish delegation to the Holy See. Yet it was the English who made such a mark here that the zone became known as the *ghetto degli Inglesi* in the 18th century. One of their favored institutions, Babington's Tea Rooms, opened on the piazza in 1893.

2 On the southern side of the Piazza is the Casina Rossa, where English Romantic poet, John Keats, spent his dying days. Today the Keats-Shelley House, at 26 Piazza di Spagna, traces the lives of both of these English poets, and has a significant collection of Romantic literature.

The focal point of Piazza di Spagna is the Fontana della Barcaccia, a frothy Baroque concoction of water and stone, the most famous work by Gian Lorenzo Bernini's father, Pietro. His "useless old boat" fountain, commissioned by Barberini pope Urban VIII, supposedly marks the spot where a boat was stranded during flooding of the Tiber in 1598.

Two Barberini family suns spout water from either end of the font, which is fed by the Aqua Virgo. In 19 B.C., the aqueduct channeled water down the adjacent Via Condotti ("street of the conduits") to Rome's first baths, the Baths of Agrippa.

Make your way up the superb flight of white travertine stairs, Scalinata di Trinità dei Monti, which wraps around the obelisk at the top in a garland of decorative marble. The most popular gathering place in Rome since the Grand Tour of 18th-century cultural pilgrims, it was designed by Francesco De Sanctis beginning in 1723. The three-tiered stairway has a total 138 steps, and is embellished with Baroque balustrades.

The steps cascade from the Piazza della Trinità dei Monti. The red granite 43-foot-high Sallustian Obelisk stands in the arch-fronted square. The views take in the Baroque dome of San Carlo ai Catinari (the third highest dome in Rome) through to St. Peter's, with a fantastic tunnel view down Via Condotti towards the Tiber riverbank

Cardinal Ferdinando
de' Medici

3 There are just a few more steps to climb to the Chiesa della Trinità dei Monti, whose ornate façade and twin bell towers were constructed with the patronage of King Louis XII in 1502, to celebrate France's invasion of Naples a few years earlier. Dedicated by Pope Sixtus V in 1585, two celebrated 16th-century frescoes by Michelangelo's mate Daniele da Volterra hang in its chapels: *The Assumption*, and *Deposition of Christ*. Ensure you take something with which to cover your shoulders even on a very hot day, otherwise you will not be able to enter.

Exit the church and descend the stairs to your right.

4 Walk north along the Viale della Trinità dei Monti to the Villa Medici, the home of the French Academy of Rome, on the Piazza della Trinità dei Monti. The villa was purchased by Cardinal Ferdinando de' Medici in 1576, eight years after Michelangelo's rival Nanni di Baccio Bigio designed it for Cardinal Giovanni Ricci as a country style *casino* on a vineyard.

The pleasure gardens of Roman general Lucius Licinius Lucullus, the horti Lucullani, were on this spot around 66 B.C. Medici re-styled it like a Florentine villa, calling on Flemish painter Giusto Utens to decorate his apartments, and overseeing the layout of the glorious gardens, which are filled with alcove fountains, gargoyles and antique statues. There are guided tours in English here every day at midday.

Leaving Villa Medici, turn right and continue north ways along the Viale della Trinità dei Monti towards the Pincio Hill.

Veer right off the sidewalk and up the Viale del Belvedere, which rises towards the entry of the gardens of the Pincio Hill.

Viale del Belvedere

5 Landscaped into a park by Giuseppe Valadier in 1809–14, the Pincio Hill was covered with gardens in ancient Rome, and known as Collis Hortulorum ("hill of gardens"). The name Pincio comes from one of the noble families who had palaces here in the 4th century A.D. The Pincio is not one of Rome's seven hills, as it lay beyond the *pomoerium*, Rome's sacred boundary.

The *belvedere* (literally beautiful vista) skirts the west-facing front of the gardens with panoramas casting over the Piazza del Popolo and Via del Corso below, to the Castel Sant'Angelo on the Tiber, the Vatican and Monte Mario.

6 The first section of the gardens between the Viale di Villa Medici and Piazza Bucaresti is a sea of sculptures. Pedestal-posed busts of illustrious Italian politicians, poets and philosophers adorn the greenery, some in a better state than others. Formal alleys are lined with pines, cypress and park benches. Along the Viale del Obelisco, is yet another of Rome's ancient Egyptian monuments, brought to Italy by the Emperor Hadrian to honor his lost love, Antinous.

The Galleria Borghese, in the park's eastern confines, is not included in this walk. Count on another couple of hours to visit Cardinal Scipione Borghese's 17th-century art collection, now owned by the state. Ticket reservation is mandatory.

The Viale di Villa Medici swerves around into the Viale Obelisco. Continue north to the Viale Valadier and turn left.

257

Monte Pincio Rome, by
Maurice Prendergast,
1898-99

The Salita del Pincio winds down through the trees towards the Piazza del Popolo, intersecting with the Viale Gabriele d'Annunzio on the Pincio Hill side of the square.

7 The sidewalk passes by the 15th-century Basilica di Santa Maria del Popolo, whose Cerasi Chapel contains Caravaggio's *Conversion of St. Paul*; two Bernini sculptures grace the Chigi Chapel. Another chapel houses the museum Il Genio di Leonardo da Vinci Museo. The exhibition includes large-scale mechanical inventions based on da Vinici's 15th-century drawings, 3D animations of his works, reproductions of his art, his preparatory and anatomical drawings, insights into his mysterious alphabet and writing technique and copies of his codices (volumes of his manuscripts and drawings, bound in parchment).

8 The Piazza del Popolo, or people's piazza, does not get its name from being a social hub, but a mistranslation of the Latin word *populus*—poplar trees, which once fringed the square. Of pivotal importance in ancient Rome, the Porta Flaminia

Then & Now

Left: *Piazza del Popolo*, by G. B. Piranesi, c.1750.

was the northern gateway to the city through the Aurelian defense walls. The gate stood just east of the current Porta del Popolo erected by Pope Pius IV in 1561.

9 Washing troughs, mules and public executions were still common when the ceremonial area became a fulcrum of Pope Sixtus V's urban planning in the 1580s, hinging on the wow-factor Flaminian obelisk, rising 87 feet in the center. The square got a Baroque revamp beginning in 1665: Bernini redesigned the gateway to greet the newly converted Swedish Queen Christina to Rome, while Carlo Rainaldi conjured up the captivating southern entrance with the twin Baroque churches, Chiesa di Santa Maria de Montesanto and Chiesa di Santa Maria dei Miracoli. The Piazza's most recent transformation came with Giuseppe Valadier's Neoclassical makeover, in 1823. He engraved distinctive semi-circular recesses into each side of the piazza, adorning them with allegorical fountains of Neptune and Triton, and statues representing the Four Seasons.

10 The *tridente*, where Via del Babuino, Via del Corso, and Via di Ripetta converge on the Piazza del Popolo, is marked by two historic people-watching cafés: Canova, where Fellini got his daily dose, and Rosati.

11 Walk south on the Via del Corso and pass the first street, Via della Fontanella. The Casa di Goethe museum at No. 18 is located in the house where the great writer lived in Rome between 1786 and 1788. The collection includes diaries and personal letters, drawings, excerpts from his work on color theory and first editions of his books. The portrait of Goethe by Andy Warhol is based on one by

the German painter Tischbein, who shared the apartment with his friend. The Casa di Goethe is open daily from 10 a.m. to 6 p.m., closed on Mondays.

12 Walk further down to south where Via del Corso meets Via della Croce. Painters Caravaggio and Orazio Gentileschi (father of painter Artemisia Gentileschi) were part of the "clique of Via della Croce" and were arrested for libel against Giovanni Baglione in 1605. The Gentileschi family moved to Via della Croce in April 1611, where Artemisia was raped by her tutor Agostino Tassi.

13 Continue two more blocks down and turn left into Via Condotti, Rome's high-end shopping street. Walk towards Piazza di Spagna and pass Via Bocca di Leone to reach Antico Caffè Greco, established at No. 86 in 1760. Illustrious guests such as Goethe, Keats, Stendhal, Byron, Liszt, and Gabriele D'Annunzio had coffee here. Goethe most likely took precisely the same route as you to reach the café.

Walk one more block to return to the Piazza di Spagna.

HIGHLIGHTS FROM THE GALLERIA BORGHESE

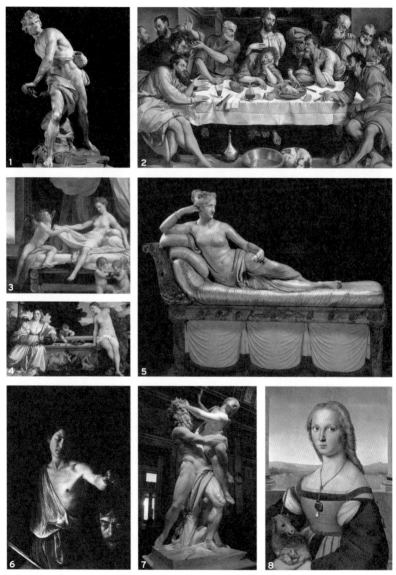

1. *David,* by Gian Lorenzo Bernini, 1623-24 **2.** *Last Supper,* by Jacopo Bassano, 1542
3. *Danäe,* by Correggio, c. 1531 **4.** *Sacred and Profane Love,* by Titian, c.1514
5. *Pauline Bonaparte,* by Antonio Canova, 1805-08 **6.** *David with the Head of Goliath,* by Caravaggio, c. 1610 **7.** *Pluto and Proserpina,* by Gian Lorenzo Bernini, 1621-22 **8.** *Lady with a Unicorn,* by Raphael, c. 1505

INDEX

BIBLIOGRAPHY

Addington Symonds, *The Life of Michelangelo Buonarroti*, University of Pennsylvania Press, Philadelphia, 2002.

Aicher, Peter, J, *Rome Alive: A Source Guide to the Ancient City*, Bolchazy-Carducci Publishers, Illinois, 1954.

Ball Platner, Samuel A *Topographical Dictionary of Ancient Rome*, Oxford University Press, London, 1929.

Barrett, Anthony A., *Caligula: The Corruption of Power*, Routledge, New York, 2000.

Bradford, Sarah, *Lucrezia Borgia: Life, Love, And Death in Renaissance Italy*, Penguin Books, 2005.

Bunson, Matthew, *A Dictionary of the Roman Empire*. Oxford University Press, New York, 1995.

Burchard, Johann, *At the court of the Borgia: being an account of the reign of Pope Alexander VI*, Folio Society, 1963.

Dio, Cassius, *Dio's Roman History, translated by Cary, Earnest*, Harvard University Press, 1989

Duffy, Eamon, *Saints & Sinners: A History of the Popes*, Yale University Press, (2nd edition) 2002.

Garrard, Mary D., *Artemisia Gentileschi: The Image of the Female Hero in Italian Baroque Art*, Princeton University Press, Princeton, 1989.

Gibbon, Edward, *The History of the Decline and Fall of the Roman Empire, Volume*, Penguin Classics (Abridged version), 2001.

Goethe, Johann Wolfgang Von, *Italian Journey: 1786-1788*, Penguin Books, London, 1992.

Graham-Dixon, Andrew, *Caravaggio: A Life Sacred and Profane*, Allen Lane, London, 2010.

Hall, Marcia. B., *Rome*, Cambridge University Press, New York, 2005.

Hall, Marcia B., (editor) *The Cambridge Companion to Raphael*, Cambridge University Press, New York, 2005.

Hopkins, Keith and Beard, Mary, *The Colosseum*, Profile Books, London, 2005

Kezich, Tullio, *Federico Fellini: His Life and Work*, Faber & Faber, New York, 2006 (NOTE translated from original title Federico: Fellini, la vita e i film, 2002)

Langdon, Helen, *Caravaggio: A Life*, Chatto and Windus, London, 1998.

Livy, *(27 B.C. History of Rome)*, Edited by Dorey, T.A., Routledge & Kegan Paul Ltd, London, 1971.

Mormando, Franco, *Bernini: His Life and His Rome*, University Of Chicago Press, 2011.

Ovid and Payne, Tom (translator), *The Art of Love (Ars Amatoria)*, Random House, London, 2012.

Robb, Peter, M: *The Man Who Became Caravaggio*, Picador, 2001

Scarre, Chris, *The Penguin Historical Atlas of Ancient Rome*, Viking, Penguin Books, London, 1995

Scarre, Chris, *Chronicle of the Roman Emperors*, Thames & Hudson, London, 2012.

Suetonius, *The Twelve Caesars*, Rives, James (editor), Graves, Robert (translator), Penguin Classics, London, 2007.

Solinas, Francesco, *Le lettere di Artemisia*, De Luca Editori d'Arte, Rome, 2011.

Tacitus, Cornelius, *The Annals*, English translation by Woodman, A.J., Hackett Publishing Company, Indianapolis, 2004.

Trollope, Anthony, *The Life of Cicero*, Harper and Brothers, New York, 1881.

Ullmann, Walter, *A Short History of the Papacy in the Middle Ages*, Routledge, New York, 2003.

Vasari, Giorgio, *The Lives of the Artists*, translated by Conaway Bondanella, Julia, and Bondanella, Peter, Oxford University Press, New York, 1998.

Virgil, *The Aeneid*, translated by John Dryden, Penguin Classics, London, 1997.

Watkin, David, *A history of Western architecture*, Laurence King Publishing, London (4th edition), 2005

Rolland, Romain, *Michelangelo*, translated by Street, Frederick, Duffield & Company, New York, 1921

IMAGE CREDITS

Page 90:
Rome, Campidoglio, © Pierrot
Heritier

Page 178:
Benito Mussolini, c. 1940 -1946,
LC-USW33-000890-ZC, Library
of Congress Prints and Photographs Division

Page 184:
Roman Holiday, Audrey Hepburn,
Gregory Peck, 1953, courtesy of
Everett Collection

Page 192:
La Dolce Vita, Anita Ekberg,
1960, courtesy of Everett Collection

Page 202:
1-1. Photo © Tamara Thiessen

Page 203:
2-1, 2. Photo © Tamara Thiessen

Page 204:
3, 4. Photo © Tamara Thiessen

Page 205:
5, 6, 7. Photo © Tamara Thiessen

Page 206:
11. Photo © Tamara Thiessen

Page 207:
11-2, 12. Photo © Tamara Thiessen

Page 212:
Palatine Hill Map. Courtesy of
Rev. Felix Just, S.J., Ph.D., Loyola
Institute for Spirituality

Page 213:
Roman Forum and Capitoline Hill
Maps. Courtesy of Rev. Felix Just,
S.J., Ph.D., Loyola Institute for
Spirituality

Page 218:
1-2. Photo © Tamara Thiessen

Page 219:
1-3, 2, 2-2. Photo © Tamara
Thiessen

Page 220:
3, 4. Photo © Tamara Thiessen

Page 221:
5, 5-2, 6. Photo © Tamara
Thiessen

Page 222:
7. Photo © Tamara Thiessen

Page 223:
8. Photo © Tamara Thiessen

Page 228:
1, 1-2, 1-3. Photo © Tamara
Thiessen

Page 229:
2, 2-4. Photo © Tamara Thiessen

Page 230:
2, 3. Photo © Tamara Thiessen

Page 231:
4, 4-2, 5. Photo © Tamara
Thiessen

Page 232:
5-3, 6, 6-2. Photo © Tamara
Thiessen

Page 233:
6-6. Photo © Pierrot Heritier

Page 236:
Photo © Tamara Thiessen

Page 238:
1, 2. Photo © Tamara Thiessen

Page 239:
2, 2-3. Photo © Tamara Thiessen

Page 240:
3, 4. Photo © Tamara Thiessen

Page 241:
Top left, 5, 6-2. Photo © Tamara
Thiessen

Page 242:
8, 9, 9-2. Photo © Tamara
Thiessen

Page 243:
10. Photo © Tamara Thiessen

Page 244:
Photo © Tamara Thiessen

Page 246:
Top. Photo © Pierrot Heritier

Page 247:
2, 3. Photo © Tamara Thiessen

Page 249:
5. Photo © Tamara Thiessen
Then & Now. Photo © Pierrot
Heritier

Page 250:
7. Photo © Pierrot Heritier

Page 251:
7. Photo © Tamara Thiessen

Page 254:
Top. Photo © Pierrot Heritier
1, 1-2. Photo © Tamara Thiessen

Page 255:
2-2. Photo © Tamara Thiessen
2-3. Photo © Pierrot Heritier

Page 256:
3, 4-3. Photo © Tamara Thiessen
4. Photo © Pierrot Heritier

Page 257:
4-4, 5, 6, 6-2. Photo © Tamara
Thiessen

Page 259:
9, 9-2, 10. Photo © Tamara
Thiessen

Other images are © Museyon or
public domain.

ABOUT MUSEYON

Named after the Museion, the ancient Egyptian institute dedicated to the muses, Museyon Guides is an independent publisher that explores the world through the lens of cultural obsessions. Intended for frequent fliers and armchair travelers alike, our books are expert-curated and carefully researched, offering rich visuals, practical tips and quality information.

MUSEYON TITLES

Pick one up and follow your interests...wherever they might go.
For more information vist **www.museyon.com**

. . . .

MUSEYON INC.
20 East 46th Street, New York, NY 10017
info@museyon.com

Publisher: Akira Chiba
Editor-in-Chief: Heather Corcoran
Cover Design: José Antonio Contreras

Maps & Illustration Design: Ray Yuen
Assistant Editor: Charlie Fish

ABOUT THE AUTHOR

Tamara Thiessen is an Australian-born author and photographer. Currently based in France—though more often on the road—her travel writing and foreign news features have appeared in publications including *The Sydney Morning Herald*, *The Toronto Globe and Mail*, *National Geographic Traveller*, *Wanderlust* and *Conde Nast Traveller*. She is the author of *the Bradt Travel Guide to Borneo* and *Cafe Life Sydney*, and a contributor to the *Eyewitness Travel Guides to Italy, France and Australia*, and to *Style City Europe*.